PRAISE FOR
The Weeping Angel
The Letters and Poems of Hubert Williams Kelley

"*The Weeping Angel* draws on one of the richest surviving collections of First World War letters to bring to life one of Uncle Sam's most remarkable—and thoughtful—doughboys.

"In this compelling book, Mary Kelley restores the human story to one corner of an inhuman war. Whether they've read one book about the war or fifty, readers will be surprised and engaged by *The Weeping Angel*."

—CHRISTOPHER CAPOZZOLA, author of *Uncle Sam Wants You: World War I and the Making of the Modern American Citizen*

"It's a wonderful book with so much compelling material…Kelley's essay, 'A Memory of Amiens,' is extraordinary. *The Weeping Angel* rescues a wonderful voice from the period, as well as the story of a remarkable regiment that is too little known.

"Kelley's description of Notre Dame, sandbagged, almost pitch-black inside, with a dusting of snow on the gargoyles is priceless. From a literary standpoint, it is interesting to watch a war poet, one not without talent—as he processes the work of [Alan] Seeger and [Rupert] Brooke and struggles to find his own voice."

—STEVEN TROUT, author of *On the Battlefield of Memory: The First World War and American Remembrance, 1919-1941.*

13 AMIENS. — La Cathédrale. — L'Ange Pleureur. — LL.

The Weeping Angel

LETTERS AND POEMS FROM WORLD WAR I FRANCE

1917–1919

HUBERT WILLIAMS KELLEY

Edited by Mary Kelley

THE WEEPING ANGEL
Letters and Poems from WWI France (1917–1919)

©2016 Mary Kelley

ISBN: 978-1-940244-70-9

Page 67 and Chapter photos by Tom field.
Photos courtesy of the Kelley family.

Published by
Willow Avenue Books

Produced and Distributed by
Boston Writers Publishing and Cooperative
www.bostonwriterspublishing.com

Printed in the United States of America

Dedicated to
Thomas L. Carroll, Jr. and Albert Benjamin Kelley
with thanks to Hubert W. Kelley, Jr. and Stephen Kelley

With special thanks to my husband, Thomas H. Field

TABLE OF CONTENTS

Foreword .... *i*

Letters and Poems from 1917 1

Letters and Poems from 1918 55

Letters from 1919 109

Undated Letter Fragments 118

Other Poems by H.W. Kelley about the war 120

A Memory of Amiens, 1931 127

Obituary 130

Afterword 132

Unpublished article for *American Magazine*
about WWII impact on France, written ca. 1945 133

PHOTOGRAPHS

Lillie Estella Williams, mother of Hubert Kelley 5

Hubert Kelley, 18 years old, 1917 9

Map of the 12th Engineers in France 33

Hubert Kelley and Fred Newby, 1918 66

Hubert Kelley, War Correspondent 66

Two views of Amiens Cathedral 67

L'Ange Pleureur, Amiens Cathedral, WWI postcard 77

Receipt dated 5/6/1918 87

Discharge letter signed by General Pershing 126

Hubert Kelley with Will Rogers, 1920's 131

Foreword

I never knew my father. He left my mother and my two brothers and me soon after I was born, and a good part of my youth was spent searching for him. I finally got to meet him when I was fifteen years old, in 1959. He died a few months later, and it was only after he died that I read many of the articles he had written, having tracked them down in the reference section of the New York Public Library. The task of transcribing these war letters and tracing his journey through France helped satisfy my yearning to know him better. He was a very good writer, so despite my disappointment in his life choices, I came to respect and admire his talent.

~~~~~~~

The two brown, battered cardboard boxes arrived at our Cambridge apartment building by U.S. mail. Both were heavy and cumbersome, but my husband and I managed to slide them into the elevator, down the hall, and into the small living room of our third-floor apartment. The cartons contained the original manuscripts of my late father's writing —letters, article drafts, poems. One of my four half-brothers had kept the collection in his attic and asked me if I wanted them before he tossed them out.

I couldn't let the writings go without seeing them, so I asked him to send them along. That night I sat on the floor to open each box and remove the contents, one page at a time. There were over a hundred letters, written from France between 1917 and 1919. Most were written in fountain pen and others were scrawled in pencil. Some had envelopes with missing stamps and all were yellowed with age. Packed in one box were half-finished drafts of magazine articles, poetry, old passports, and faded military records. It was all a jumble and it had the smell of mildew.

The letters immediately transported me back in time, but they were not in chronological order and soon I was lost in confusion about where and when they were written. Some letters were tattered with fragments of writing, others were covered with coffee stains or cigarette burns. Through the dates on the letters and some guesswork, I was gradually able to put them into order. They told the story of a young soldier's journey from basic training at Camp Gaillard near St. Louis, Missouri, in 1917 to the battles of northern France.

A year later, on a journey to Kansas City to visit the Kansas City Star newspaper where my father had worked, I discovered a book by Colonel John A. Laird, the commander of my father's regiment, The History of the Twelfth Engineers, U.S. Army, written in 1919. The World War I Museum there contains a treasure trove of information about the war, including this book and collections of prose and poetry. By comparing the dates in Laird's detailed account of those war years, I was able to place almost every letter and understand what events and battles were taking place as my father wrote home. I have annotated the letters accordingly.

Later I traveled to Amiens, my father's place for short furloughs and restoration, to see the site of the beautiful cathedral and its many memorials and statues. There, buried in the back looking over a tomb, is a small sculpture called The Weeping Angel, which is often referred to in his letters. Amiens has dedicated itself to the remembrance of The Great War, and walking through its streets and visiting exhibitions showing the battle sites and the devastation of the Somme brought me closer to what he saw as a young man going to war.

~~~~~~

Hubert Williams Kelley, the fourth of six children, was a sophomore in high school in Kansas City, Missouri, when the war began on July 28, 1914. Three years later, when Kelley graduated from Central High, a slight but very bright young man, he immediately went to enlist in the army engineer corps because American troops were not in combat yet. He was not alone—the War Department had coined the slogan, "Join the Engineers and be in France in 60 days." It was an enticing offer to young men from the Midwest, and hundreds answered the call. The only prerequisite for joining the army engineers was some experience working on railway lines. Kelley had none, and his small frame and low weight were not assets. Thinking quickly after the recruiting officer's initial rejection, he said that he could play the bugle. Since the army needed buglers, the officer signed him up. Kelley could not play the bugle or any other instrument at all, but he was determined and persuasive.

During the war, he became known as the regimental poet of the 12th Railway Engineers. Several of his wartime poems were published in the New York Herald and in the Paris edition of *Stars and Stripes*. After returning home, he became a news reporter for the Kansas City Star, and in the 1930s he moved east to write and edit for Crowell Collier Publications. For several years he was editor of the *American Magazine*, for which he also wrote until 1950.

When he joined the army, he was excited to be going on what he called "a great adventure." He wrote that it would be a once-in-a-lifetime experience, and from the beginning, he reassured his family that this was preparing him for "life." When he went back to Europe as a reporter during the Second World War, his articles and columns reflected the pain of seeing another wartime.

My father corresponded with the living members of the 12th until he died in 1959. During 1944, he served as a war correspondent and was briefly trapped at the Battle of the Bulge. In the mid-1950s, he sent for his official army record with his enlistment and discharge dates, and it was included with his letters. He was always looking for new story ideas, and even then, he was making inquiries of other soldiers about the flu epidemic that hit so many troops during WW I and which he had escaped.

Infested with lice night and day, living in unbearably close contact with your fellow soldiers and then watching them get blown up or horribly wounded, wondering why you were still alive but also wondering why you were not at the front line—these were just some of the realities that my father and many other American soldiers came to live with.

But his letters were filled with humor and vivid descriptions about life in wartime and his fellow soldiers: Miles Standish, overweight colonial descendant; getting lost after a Frenchman purposely gave him wrong directions; trying to make pudding with evaporated milk; and later wrestling with ideas of God and religion. As his time there progressed, we see his growing recognition that his work was writing and that he took pride in it.

Always sent from "somewhere" in France, most letters were written to his mother back in Kansas City, with a few to his father and sisters, Ouida and Connie, the two oldest, and Kathleen and Grace, the two youngest, who were still at home. There was also mention of his high school teachers Miss Boggess and Miss Harriman, who sent him books to read in between marches. His older brother, Clarence, was also in France but far away, so news about him came from his mother back home. Just after the Armistice, Hubert and Clarence met up on a train in Grenoble, an incident recounted in a missive written in 1919 when both were awaiting discharge.

Letters home did not reflect actual daily realities or events. Cheerful, "I-am-fine" missives with "thanks for the package" or "I got a letter from so-and-so" when he had just marched eleven miles all night in mud and cold and his feet were bleeding and shells were dropping all around say it all. One can only imagine how this kind of experience affected these young soldiers, at least the ones lucky enough to return alive.

Kelley remained a Private and a Bugler throughout the war. He was among the very first troops to arrive in France, ahead of most units in the American Expeditionary Forces. The 12th Engineers was a light-gauge railway unit, laying their own miniature track and carrying ordnance and other heavy materials right up to the front lines.

I have added the poetry he wrote during the war to the letters, as well as some of his later poetry and essays at the end. The letters begin in June 1917, soon after his high school graduation when he joined the army and began basic training at Camp Gaillard. The 12th Engineers were living in large floating barracks on the river.

Letters from 1917

Camp Gaillard
June 9, 1917

Dear Folks: I have been hustling since five o'clock this morning, and consequently have little time to write as it is near evening and I have a bath to take, etc. Yesterday I was off all day while the day before I was on fatigue – barracks orderly. Hereafter I was to be exempt from fatigue, as I started bugling this morning – that is, just practicing under Chief Bugler Morgan.

This afternoon we took a four-mile hike down the river. At the conclusion of the hike we washed our feet in the Mississippi, and the Captain came around and examined them. He is a prince – our Captain. When we were vaccinated he went at the head of the line, and after his shot, went out of the hospital boat in the hot sun of the parade ground to help the men who felt faint. When a fellow fainted he would be there to catch him. Fortunately we had very little trouble. I had none at all. My arm is all right.

Captain McGeehan sent me to the non-commissioned officer's school with the picked men to-day. I heard nothing new.

There are certainly some good fellows in our company. College men some of them. Tell Bunting, pop, that I met his friend Harry Mudd. Good fellow. Dunn is great. Herman Nagel is in Company O. With love, Hubert

Haven't heard from home – Address, Hubert W. Kelley, Company D, 2nd Engineers, Camp Gaillard, St. Louis

Camp Gaillard,
July 10, 1917 (on YMCA stationery)
Dear Folks, I am all in and am going to beat it for my bunk in a few minutes. I've had a rather strenuous day of it. We roll out at five o'clock, line up for roll call, wash in cold water for mess; consume bacon and – potatoes, coffee, bread etc.; then report for exercise after strenuous gymnastics. We rest fifteen minutes, then back to drill. I usually am in file closer [*sic*], instructor, chief or subordinate "hepper." At nine fifteen I report to the bugling squad and we go down in the woods and practice till 11:15. Then I am off until 1:20. During the interval we wash our faces, clothes, teeth or whatever demands an aquatic massage. At one thirty we take a hike which lasts until about four, when I report to Lieut. Smith for "non-com" school. At five Russell and I go to the head-quarters boat, and while the color guard stands on the upper deck blow "Retreat" and "To the Color" with the squad. Then nothing to do until tomorrow.

At present only two of the buglers can blow well enough to go on guard, that is to go into the guard tent with his company's guard mount for twenty-four hours and blow all the calls through the day and night. When we are not on guard we blow only several of the calls together.

This is a picturesque place at night. When the moon is full, we sit on deck and hear some of the fellows sing. We have some good singers. Sometimes big steamboats Orleans bound cough down the river, and rock our bunks with waves from the saddle wheel. When we get ready to crawl from in our barracks room is one grand uproar [*sic*]. These Irish railroaders are witty in a sense. Their rail road terms are comical. They call me a "high-wheeler," or did so for a while after I took them across the field twenty-seven times. I didn't count them but they swore they did.

I am sending my clothes tomorrow. The shirt is rather dirty. I didn't wash it although I am running a personal Chinese laundry in a wash pan.

The men have their rifles and bayonets now and will soon have the rest of their equipment. Thank the stars I don't carry a rifle. I carry or will carry a six shooter tied around my leg. The officers and buglers carry them. (Incidentally I am exempted from all detail and fatigue thereafter.)

I have heard nothing from anybody up to date. My address is: Hubert W. Kelley, Company D, 2nd Engineers, Camp Gaillard, St. Louis, Mo. Put it all in.

Has Ouida gone yet? Give me Connie's address. A Kansas City Star would be appreciated. With love to all, Hubert

(No date or salutation – first page missing:
Written at Camp Gaillard)

Tonight our guards must walk in the rain, for it is pouring. I just met Herman Nagel pacing his post. The men are carrying rifles tonight, and a shiny wicked bayonet is fixed on the ends of them. This is the first time they have resorted to such drastic means of protection. (ha!)

Yesterday we had inspection. I stood with the rest for two hours in the hot sun. The Colonel and his staff walked down the lines and inspected them and the Captain made note of their criticisms. The officers are not exactly euphemistic in their treatment of the men. The Major is likely to jerk a rifle from a man's hands, look down the barrel of it, pronounce it disgracefully dirty, and rebuke the owner of it without ceremony. A note is made of the untidy me. My name was not taken – thank the stars! The Captain kindly suggested that I clean some of the oil out of my automatic, however. (That reminds me, neither of our higher officers Captain McGeehan or Lieutenant Smith use tobacco. That is something rare around this place.)

Yesterday afternoon the Engineer's Club of St. Louis presented our regimental colors. The first infantry band came out and played for us. The whole regiment was assembled on the parade ground. The bugle (or bungle) squad was assembled behind the band. The colors certainly were inspiring as they swept down the ranks in the hands of the color sergeant. You cannot imagine what a new lustre [*sic*] it added to the regiment.

I have made acquaintances since I came here – some worthwhile and some I do not care to continue. Last night I had a very interesting conversation with a man. He was certainly a character.

He was born in England, attended school in London, where he boarded. His father was wealthy and severe. Every month he sent the boy a generous allowance, but the boy gambled it away. Finally at the end of his career in school, the boy received enough to come home on, and to buy what trifles he might wish. Instead of going home, he went to Liverpool, where he stayed for three weeks. Everyday he stayed, his fear of returning was greater. Finally he embarked on a British Marine and came to America as a stowaway. He hasn't heard from home in twelve years. He has worked on every road from Alaska to the Gulf almost – has been in several wrecks, has had his skull fractured (maybe that's what's the matter with him), has had his legs fractured, has scars all over him, and is still here. He told me that after the war [is] over, that he was going to Liverpool to find his folks (they do not live there, his brother is a custom's house officer there – or was when he left). The most remarkable thing about the man is that he seems to be religious. How sincere he is I do not know. He has been a Catholic but is now a "non-partisan." There are millions of Catholics here. He gave me a long lecture on fortitude – told me, that if I were critiqued by the Colonel for any break in bugling I might make, to realize that I was suffering for the Lord Jesus Christ. He later said that he had put up a "damned poor showing at inspection." I didn't know whether to laugh or not. I'm going to talk to him some more. He is very interesting – I do not know whether he is honest or no. He has some marked eccentricities which would make as good a character as our mutual friend "Micawber."

I have been interested in many others here. There is one "old belly-acher" here who sleeps in the aisle of our bunk room. He is built like a spoilt baby – he uses the most whining profanity of any discontented wretch I ever heard. I dislike profanity very much, but I at least like to hear it spoken as if it were meant. "If you must cuss, cuss like a man." Good motto. We have one monster here, ex-Captain of a college football team. He is just out of school. I was told (by his majesty himself) to call him "Dave." I call him "little Davy" for short.

If you have any extra handkerchiefs, I could use them. I think you have some of my new B.V.D.s left. If you have any of the aforesaid left, they would be appreciated. Don't buy anything for goodness sake. If you have them on hand, send them to this address. If we are gone, you need have no fears – they will be forwarded. If you have a gumdrop handy, put it in the bundle – if you send one.

Understand, I am at no inconvenience whatsoever. I am able to keep myself clean. I do my own washing too. This is evidenced by the absence of all epidermis from one of my knuckles.

There are some wretches in the tent eating a variety of food. Think of it. They have friends in St. Louis, who come down to the camp and bring such unheard of things as olives and fried chickens. The Martin brothers got an angelfood cake yester-eve, and went divvy with me. IT was some cake.

Well, I must cease and kid someone else a while. With love, Hubert

Lillie Estella Williams, Hubert's mother

Camp Gaillard, Mo
(Sometime in June 1917)

Dear Mother: I have been here on the Mississippi two days, and have come to the conclusion that it will either kill me or make a man of me. We drill in the hot sun about six hours a day, and have the rest of the time to ourselves. Not to lie idle, however, for we have our own washing to do, and we must keep our bunks in a sanitary condition. I sleep in one about 3 stories up – right against the roof of a house boat. Excuse the digressions, for I am chuck full of things to tell, and I hardly know where to begin.

I took my final exam today and almost was exempted on account of my weight, but since I am a musician, and musicians are scarce, I was allowed to stay. So I am safe in camp, and expect to remain so until something unexpected turns up. I was measured for my uniform last night, and will be equipped tomorrow, when I will send home my duds. (Just like I pulled them off.)

Now as to my work, I have been drilling rookies all afternoon, and laid two booze-fighters out. They were almost overcome by the heat. I am certainly on good terms with the officers and me here, even if I have drilled my men harder than any one around here this afternoon. I am not bragging; they admit it. The Captain drills most of the men, and when a couple of new squads come into camp, he turns them over to one of the corporals (there are two), to one of the prospective sergeants, or to me. I drilled three squads for three hours, and, as I say, two men were almost overcome by heat, and would have been had I not excused them. This morning and yesterday afternoon I drilled with the company marching on the left wing as a file closer and drum. We have none here, so I use my voice in a sonorous "hep! Hep!" or "one, two, three, four," etc.; military experience certainly counts up here, and almost guarantees an officership. However, I suppose I will be used as a bugler. Anyway I do not think I am old enough to get a chevron.

Some of these boys around here think I'm an officer; salute and ask questions on military tactics, but I refer them to the officers in charge. Don't want to incur their antipathy, of course. Some of these men are too _____ in their ankles to right face. We get them out individually and drill them till they know the movement. They grunt, sweat, and cuss, but they must do it. We have a guard house, where they are feeding a guardsman on bread and water for nineteen days. Well, I suppose you want to know something about the camp.

(A rudimentary drawing is part of the letter.)

The edge of Granite City, Illinois

Mississippi River   Island

_____||_____/ our boat barracks

Bank   (Map)

This is a very unartistic picture but will give you an idea of our position on the river. The parade grounds are up on the banks. They are grassy and very rough. Sometimes we drill on the dive way, about a half a mile over. Occasionally, we'll take hikes down the river, I suppose. We have clean quarters and wholesome food, so the men will be kept in good condition.

Tomorrow I think we'll get my first shot of typhus serum, though I am not sure. Don't worry about it, for about a thousand others are surviving it. That makes me think I will. I met J.S. Taylor in the Medical Corps, and he seems to be a very good fellow. (Tell Grace to send me that wrist watch when it comes. I think I can use it without danger of being robbed. Somebody else may get one when they see me with one. (Don't get shocked! I stand up in pretty well up here.)

I met Dick Dunn, and he's a regular watchdog over my welfare. He is certainly a prince of a fellow.....

I hope everybody is well. Tell Junior I found Tommy Turtle cold and stiff upon the bank of the river today. I have plenty of cash though we got no pay. There is no place to spend it but the Y.M.C.A. confectionary. We cannot go to St. Louis. It is ten miles away. If I need anything will write for it. Address: (He gives it again.)

With love to all, Hubert

Camp Gaillard, Mo
July 11, 1917

Dear Folks, I was delighted to receive Ma's, Clarence's, and Connie's letters. I had about given [up] hope of every hearing from home. I would like to have Connie's address so that I might write to her.

They are working us like the deuce. This is what is known as intensive training, and, from the hikes they are imposing, rather extensive. I was unable to drill today as my foot was sore. I fell down the back steps about one-sixteenth of the way, and knocked the skin off the knuckle of my big toe. Nothing serious, only extremely inconvenient, or convenient when you consider the afternoon tramp through dust and cinders. I stayed home; took a bath under the ice-cold shower, and felt fine generally. I went to bugle and "non-com" school though.

There are many interesting things happening around here. Yesterday Miles Standish, a some what obese descendent of the old colonial family, offered the Capt. one of his extra gun belts. The Captain gave one long drawn sniff of contempt and walked off. Miles is certainly put out. The Capt. thought he was trying to boot-lick. He won't stand for any thing of that kind; he is absolutely fair and indiscriminate [*sic*]. The men admire him for it, and, as one fond devotee said, they would go to h____ for McGeehan. Miles Standish did not mean anything, however. He is a fat round-faced, blue-eyed good- natured fellow who expects to do photography work in a biplane. One brakeman said, though, that no aviator would take up that tub o' meat. The funniest thing yet happened on guard the other night. Part of it is true, and the rest is the humorous "concoction" of these Irish roughnecks. The relief squad approached and gave the answer to the rookie sentinel's challenge, where upon he said, "Advance squab [*sic*] and give the counter-balance," meaning, of course, advance and give the countersign. Another sentinel, instead of saying, "advance and be recognized," said, "advance and be identified." Another said, "Advance boy; I know yuh." Pretty good, eh?

I am sorry Junior was sick, and that Ouida is leaving. Tell papa I met one of his old customers, Claude E. Henderson, a bridge foreman. Dunn is going to write to papa.

I'll have to quit, I think. Some woman is piping a ballad to the poor, forlorn soldiers in the __ tent, and I'll have to stop and listen. I've seen only one woman worth looking at since I've been here. She had the countenance of that Madonna which hangs in the parlor. George, Clair Martin's brother, stared and stared, and wondered at the sympathy of her eyes. (Here he drew three stars.) Most of these girls who come around camp are as superficial as a stick of spearmint. They are pert, painted, and silly!

The Captain expects us to leave in two or three weeks. We have much to learn. That woman is singing "poor buttermilk" or rather _____ – in the basso of a dying cat, so here goes —

With love, Hubert Write soon—

Camp Gaillard
July 12, 1917

Dear Folks: Last I wrote you a long letter addressed and stamped it, but became interested in a fluent speaker of Francais and left it lying on the table. Maybe some kind hearted private picked it up and mailed it.

I received my second injection of serum today, so please excuse the handwriting. My arm, like all the others, is pretty stiff. Several fellows flopped, but they are booze fighters and suckers of the coffin nail for the most part.

Mooney wrote me a discourse on the things that are and are to be. When I came, I wrote to Uncle Hamp. He answered with a special delivery, two of his pictures, and several of his titles. He seems to think I had done the right thing. I was certainly glad to hear from him. I sent him a clipping from the "St. Louis Star" stating that we are to leave by August first. There are many rumors that we are to leave by Saturday week. But that is to another camp either in Pennsylvania or Georgia. A wire at the hospital states that our medical crew is to be fully equipped in New York City. I do not know whether they are to accompany us. So you see how diversified reports are.

Today we were equipped with shelter tents, ponchos, knap-sacks, canteen, cartridge belts, blanket rolls, and first aid kits. The men already have rifles and bayonets. The rifles are Kraz-Joren and consequently may not be for active service. I do not know. I have not yet been issued my six-shooter. Russell has his but he lives in the office.

They are about to put up a moving picture curtain in the tent, so I must stop and see the show. You know how these soldiers must have their entertainment. They are yelling now at a barbarous prize fight being promoted out side.

I am certainly gaining the desired experience with a vengeance. I learn new things every day. I have no doubts but I can make a minister of some practical knowledge when I get out of the army. I don't tell the boys that though, for they have little respect for a preacher. The other day some brakeman said, "There's a boy upstairs reading his [B]ible" (I don't know who he was), and his ___ answered, "Somebody getting scared, I guess."

These men, some of them, are good, wholehearted men, but some of them are not worth shooting. I think George Martin and I are the only two in our barracks who do not smoke. None of us drink, for there is nothing to drink but iced tea, and we chipped in for that. Well – ta-ta.

With love, Hubert. Write soon and lots of it.

Hubert W. Kelley, 1917

(Camp Gaillard, undated)

I am glad to hear we are to move. A small house will not be nearly so lonesome. Do you think so? I have just been watching Honeywell's balloon over St.

Louis. He flew this morning, but descended when rain came up.

(Harry E. Honeywell was a famous balloonist who won many awards. The balloonist school in St. Louis trained soldiers to fly in the war effort in WW I.)

Today I met one Arch M. Brown from Poteau and immediate vicinity. He worked at "Heavenor" I think he called it that. His "quid" rather muffled his enunciation. I met another fellow who knew glass and Whitebread [?] in Hurts-horne. It was interesting to meet a few of such clansmen. One fellow in the corps went to school in Fayettsville. I met these fellows while we were march-ing to Boden [Baden?]. That hiking is hard on the feet.

I understand I am to get $33, or a first class private's pay while I bugle. Some class, eh? I had a chance to take an aristocratic job the other day, but I didn't. Colonel Adams, who just arrived, wanted a porter out of Co. D. One man volunteered, and is now Colonel's orderly.

Well, it is getting dark and I must quit. We are going to have a dance tomor-row. We are not, rather – they are, the dance is in honor of the 12th Engineers. Our name has now been changed. We are no longer the Second. We are still railway men, however. Address my mail as you always have.

I am sending you a very poor photograph taken on top of our boat. I had no equipment whatsoever, was in the shirt sleeves, and look like the devil in general. It is rather picturesque overlooking the Mississippi.

Too dark to write, Ta Ta, HW Kelley, alias Hubert (I feel facetious)

Camp Gaillard
July 14, 1917

Dear Mother: It is gray and drizzly, and drill for this morning was aban-doned. Nobody cares much, for all recuperation possible to be had is appreci-ated. Yesterday, we were sick dogs, for we had our second injection of pro-phylaxis. That is the worst. I feel fine now though. But yesterday (he draws three stars) Good Night! We were sea-sick, as it were. Every time a steam boat passed, she sent waves which rolled our barracks into convulsions. It was fierce. (Excuse the other side. I blotted it with a wet blotter.)

I have heard many rumors that we leave here next week. Tuesday or Wednesday. I do not know whether they are grounded or not. The Captain of Co. A told his men that they would spend their last Sunday in camp tomorrow. I hope he is right. We have also heard rumors of going to Siberia, instead of France. I do not know. I don't care, for when things of such magnitude are being considered, I cannot choose.

Last night I went to Baden, a small town three miles from here. Got a hair cut and an egg malted milk. I had forgotten what an egg tasted like. (Just had to stand up at attention. This is inspection day at camp, and the Colonel and staff came through.)

Must close – Write soon. Received Ouida's letter. With love, Hubert

Camp Gaillard
July 10, 1917

Dear Mother: I just received your letter accompanied by Connie's, the wrist watch, and the K.C. Star which I am getting regularly at somebody's expense. I was certainly disgusted to hear of Edgar's premature venture into matrimony. He is too young to tie up to what he did without serious consideration.

I was given my official appointment as bugler today. It was posted on the bulletin board with several other announcements. Dick Dunn is now a sergeant. Good for Dick! Along with my appointment I was given a forty-five automatic Colt which hangs heavily at my side as I write. Our bugles are only about ten inches long and strike very high notes. I do not like their tone in the least.

I have been hearing some more substantial information considering our departure. The dentist says that we will not be here four more days. The Captain said we would be given the rest of our equipment at New York City. It will be issued on the way over.

(The letter ends here without a sign-off.)

Camp Gaillard
July 21, 1917

Dear Folks: I will take this opportunity to drop a line. We have had inspection all morning, and standing at attention has almost paralyzed my frame. We have been wrapped in heavy marching order packs, knapsacks, etc. They inspected our guns. I suppose I told you about my seven shooting automatic.

I received Papa's and Grace's letters and was certainly glad to get them. (Gee, it is dusty in this tent. They are cleaning it out. Last night we had a regimental dance here, and a large canvas has been spread on the floor.)

It is generally conceded that we will be out of here about Monday. The mess-sergeant is willing to bet we will be on board next Saturday. I don't know about that. They are packing now, breaking camp every where. We are going to Hoboken, New Jersey, by way of Toledo, Ohio. Thence we will sail to France.

We are to be given new clothes in the east. Take all this with a grain of salt, as I don't know anything for certain. Write often – it will be forwarded. (Dick Dunn wrote to pop and wants an answer.)

With love to all, Hubert (got a letter from Fidell)

(Fidell was married to Ouida, his oldest sister.)

Camp Gaillard

July 22, Sunday

Dear Folks: Today our trucks, motorcycles, and baggage were shipped to New York City (c/o Supt's of Transports, 12th Engineers) Those of our men accompanied the motor cycles and cars. There are several cars of ammunition waiting on the tracks around the curve. Our own company was on guard there. We are to leave immediately. When, I do not know, but the Captain said it would be Wednesday or Thursday. From what I have overheard among the officers, we are to be shipped on our arrival in New York. We expect to be in France in two weeks. The men are certainly enthusiastic over the out-look. I am, for it is a wonderful opportunity. The U boats are no impediment. We have convoys of destroyers, which can cope with any submarine, I feel confident. In a year or so, maybe before, I shall come out fuller and richer with experience than the average man of my age.

Last night I went on guard for the first time – that is, bugler guard. At ten o'clock, while the camp was still and dim with that soft purple which starry evenings know, I took my station at one end of the camp on the bank of the river, and Russell took his place about a quarter of a mile away – far down at the opposite end of the line of boats. He blew taps, and one by one the lurid yellow lights flickered and died in the windows, and as he finished, I took it up and repeated it. The notes ring so they echo on the sides of the boats and the lap and lash of the river seems almost melancholy as one finishes. We slept in the guard tent, just rolled up in our blankets and dropped off to sleep. I was awakened several times as the sentinels changed watches, but one doesn't mind that. There is a certain touch of romance in the clash of bayonets, the confused babble of voices, and the hoarse commands at mid-night. It is so vague, so much like a dream, that one rather appreciates the experience of it. *(Letter ends here.)*

Camp Gaillard
July 23, 1917

Dear Folks: Another rain has set in and I will utilize the spare time before I get my fourth shot in the arm. I have just finished "beef," and was pleased to find two letters awaiting me there. I received Mama's cheery missive, and Clarence's announcement of a trip to Honolulu en route to Russia. It seems that he hears rumors too.

I am practically certain that we will leave Thursday. Pleasant anticipation, isn't it? I cannot realize that I am to leave New York Harbor – maybe Monday. And France –won't it be wonderful? We are to work in the devastated parts. And champagne and wine – but I have solemnly resolved to leave it strictly alone. It is no trouble for me to be abstinent here – it won't there [*sic*]. But a man deserves very little credit for being decent, I suppose. It merely shows a marble disposition. I believe I have one. Curses!!

There went the bugler and the boys are buckling on their harness. I must get out of my bunk and dally forth in the rain for battalion drill.

I got the stamps. Good bye, Hubert

P.S. Here is our regiment. Note the river and some of the boats. *(He includes a primitive drawing.)*

~~~~~~~

July 26, 1917: The 12th left Camp Gaillard on trains from the Chain of Rocks Pumping Plant. It was very hot. Each man carried a 70-pound pack and wore a heavy woolen uniform. There were eleven cars in the first train. The men spent the night on the train in Jersey City, then went by ferry to Pier 54 of the Cunard Steamship Line. No men were to be seen on deck or at any porthole until the ship cleared Sandy Hook. So there was no appearance of life on decks except for the ship's officers and crew.[1]

(Postcard from 1917)

We land[ed] in Jersey City late last night and will probably embark in a short time. I will write as often as possible. I am in fine condition and anxious

---

[1] *History of the Twelfth Engineers, U.S. Army*, by Colonel John A. Laird, First Edition, 1919 p.9.

for the trip to France. These experiences are so wonderful that I cannot begin on a postcard. Hubert

July 28, 1917

Dear Mother: I am sitting on the deck of the liner R.M.S. Carmania, a British mail ship. It is one of the steel plated monsters in the same class as the Lusitania! We have just embarked. When we are to sail, I do not know. The sooner the better. We are to have a convoy of battle ships I think. Do not be worried. It will come out all right in the end.

We certainly had a wonderful trip across country. We slept in Pullmans, and our kitchen crew manned the mess rooms in the baggage car. We went through Columbus Ohio, Indianapolis, Pittsburg [*sic*], Philadelphia, Jersey City, and finally after a little trip down the Hudson in a giant tug boat, we have embarked on our transport.....

(Letter is torn here, mentions shouts, describes harbor, yacht turning around in the water confused, looking for something they cannot find.)

Across the way is another steel-plated liner like ours. I think it is to carry the Seventeenth Engineers from Atlanta, Georgia. They have been loading their baggage all morning.

They are just telling me that any letters with information of importance will be destroyed so I think I close my mouth. I am in good health. My hopes are high so rest easy, With love to all, Hubert

> *The R.M.S. Carmania landed in Liverpool, England, on August 12, 1917. Breakfast was served by the Scot's Guards and there were a few hours of drill. They detrained at Waterloo Station on August 15.* [2]

England
August 14, 1917

Dear Mother: I am safe in England, I am in the best of health, and expect to remain so for some time to come. I know you are worried beyond all reason, but you must be patient if my letters are few. I do not think I can receive any mail until I reach France. How soon we shall go I do not know. There are many rumors, but the army is a veritable hot box of falsity. Possibly you hear many

---

[2] Ibid., p. 14

terrifying reports, but until they are verified by Washington you may rest assured that they have no foundation.

England is certainly a beautiful country. It is not the wild beauty of America, but it is a cultivated, neat, clean cut beauty, the result of hundreds of years of plowing and pruning – of careful, precise gardening. The villages are crowded, but they are so neat with narrow lanes, square gardens of pink and purple, and their infinite numbers of thorn and yew hedges, that one becomes attached to them at first sight. The houses are all of one style; all have the high sloping roof of orange tyle, many chimneys, and a few small windows.

The people are certainly interesting. It is hard to understand, that is, their dialect, but they have remarkable vocabularies. Some of these ignorant Sammies cannot understand them. Most of the women and old men (they, together with the children, are all of the inhabitants left in the towns and cities) are rather conservative, and are pathetically serious. They realize the fullest burden of the war. Our men are light hearted. Last night as our regiments marched into camp along a white rock road, I could see little groups of women and children huddled along the way in the dim light, and I know that those people were almost overcome with emotion. I heard several sobs, and heard one woman exclaim in a whisper, "Isn't it grand?"

I forgot to tell you about the railroads. They remind one of a trip to toy land. The freight cars are about 10 feet long, and carry about twelve tons. The passenger cars are first, second (I saw none of these) and third. We rode in the last. They are divided into compartments entered from the side and holding about ten. They are very comfortable. Of course the engines are small, almost like the Forest Park locomotive (I believe they are somewhat larger). Each has a name – Lodestar, Lord of Cork, etc. They certainly run easily. A start or stop is scarcely perceptible. The driver, stoker, and guard (engineer, fireman, and conductor) are certainly jolly chaps, don't you know, but they talk so bally queer.

There are many Belgians in England. Little refugees ran by the train at the stations and asked for "two bob," "hapennies," and "thripny-bits" – (two pence, half-pennies, three penny pieces). A "jimmy o' goblin" is a half crown, I think. You would certainly get muddled over the change. It is Chinese to most of us.

By the time this reaches you, I shall be in France and Grace and Kathleen will be in school. Strange, isn't it. But this is a school for me. The English boys go at eighteen per force; and one old salt told me his boy left at fifteen, and served his seventeenth in the trenches. This is a great cause – the Allies need all the men possible. They need me.

I should like to hear from Clarence. Tell him to write me from Russia – or

Oshkosh. My address is as I gave you when I left —
American Expeditionary Force in France, Co. D. 12th Eng. Bugler H.W. Kelley.
You can put this in its correct order.

———

I suppose Connie came home on the fifth of August. I thought about her on
that day (his ship was at sea en route to England). I wish I could tell you more,
but someday, perhaps I can tell it "avec le livre."

Well, I must quit (with respects to the censor). I shall write more soon.
Au revoir.

*On August 15, the Twelfth led the historic march into London.
Foreign troops had not been in London since 1066 when William the
Conqueror arrived from Normandy to take the British throne. The
new American troops were reviewed in front of Buckingham Palace
by King George V and Queen Alexandra with Prime Minister Lloyd
George. Women and children with three years of lost men, sons and
husbands, watched with solemn faces and hope as they greeted the
newly arrived Twelfth.[3]*

*"It was not, in the superficial sense, a picturesque procession.
But it was intensely moving, very inspiring; and there could be no
greater message of cheer and consolation in a time of war-weariness
than the message in the eyes and gait of every American soldier who
passed through our city yesterday. That message was, 'We mean to see
it through.'"[4]*

*Clarence Woodbury in the American Legion Magazine wrote,
"Flowers were strewn in our path, Cockney girls showered us with kiss-
es and Woodbine cigarettes, and the King's own butlers served us meat
pies and bottles of ginger beer."[5]*

*On August 15, on order from the American Expeditionary Forces
headquarters in Paris, the 12th Engineers were transferred to British control.[6] They were attached to the British Third Army, building
and maintaining railroad track lines. There was speculation as to why
the Twelfth was transported in two boats instead of one until one of*

---

[3] Ibid., p. 14–16.

[4] *London Daily Chronicle*, August 16, 1917, as quoted in the *History of the Twelfth Engineers*, Ibid. p.18.

[5] "They Fought with Picks and Shovels," *American Legion Magazine*, March 1959

[6] Laird, *History of the Twelfth Engineers*, p.24.

the British officers explained, "That is done in crossing the Chanel to Boulogne, so that if one boat is torpedoed and lost there will still remain an organization of sufficient mourners to tell what a damn fine bunch the others had been..." [7]

The 12th detrained at Roisel on August 21 and marched to their pup tent camp east of Montigny Sugar Mill. They could hear the sounds of the shells, the howitzers, and the machine guns. Sleep was out of the question that first night. They had watched from trains the desolate landscape of the war where three years of battle had left scars and leveled villages, with only crumbling walls remaining, trenches running in all directions. [8]

France

August 30, 1917

Dear Connie: Perhaps you may be interested to know that I have Miss Jones's (Whittier School) brother for a "bunkie." We did not know of the coincidence until yesterday when we were discussing our sisters, and, incidentally, some other people's sisters, etc. You may tell Miss Jones that Wiley E. Jones is somewhere in France with your own "kid brother."

I have been knocking about a bit with a young "chap" from Bradford, England. He is as genial as any man I have ever met. He, among other "Tommies," plans to come to the United States after the war. I asked him to stay with me when he came to KC and he readily agreed. Of course it is only romantic to think of such things – they are too far removed from a possibility of reality. He has seen service at all the important drives made by the British, and has been "over the top" three times.

You should hear the expressions he uses. They are only typical British phrases. He was telling me that he had written home concerning a "jolly good chap from America." He frequently uses that phrase "carry on" which is a coinage of the war. Everything is "carry on" – a good billet (bunk), a dixie of porridge, a pair of putters.

He is always talking about going back to "Blighty" before he "goes over" again.

It seems strange to hear these Tommies sing our popular songs in this desolate place. The other night I heard a Tommy splashing through the muck in his

[7] Ibid., p. 26.
[8] Ibid., p. 32.

steel-plated brogans, singing "All I can think of tonight is a field all snowy white." These Englishmen can sing too.

I believe that a dialect will originate in the vicinity of large bodies of soldiers here. I have noticed that the French _____ speak a combination of English and French in most of their conversations – not only with us, but between themselves. The English use French in their speech with the nonchalance of a Crusader. Such phrases as "tre bon," "je ne pence pas," "bon nui, avez-vous," etc., are current. They are usually pronounced in English, and cannot be spelled by the user.

Give my love to all and take a bit for yourself. Don't make yourself sick teaching school, and be easy on the poor little "diables" under you. Your brother, Hubert *(Connie was three years older than Hubert.)*

In France

September 4, 1917

Dear Mother: At last the sun has come into a clear blue sky which is more characteristic of France than the gray, drizzling, muddy weather we have had for so long. The moon is full now and rises pale and silvery behind the deep green fir trees over the hill. It is a sight to be remembered.

I am usually down in the ruins at sunset.[9] My friend, the Tommy, and I have established a rendezvous in a derelict boiler, and there we meet to cook our evening porridge after mess. He is the cook, his pal the consumer and I am connoisseur and capitalist. The chef is a real cook, too, for he cooked a seven course dinner for officers up the line. This porridge, alias oatmeal, has appealed to my appetite ever since I made its acquaintance aboard ship.

Speaking of the sea trip reminds me of a very peculiar individual I met while on my way across. One night while Russell and I were in our bunks discussing the things that are and the things that are not, a young fellow from another regiment walked up and introduced himself as Allison from the mountains of North Carolina. He reminded me very much of our mutual friend, "Uriah Heep." His eyes were glittery, his hands clammy, and his constant flow of words, for which he never seemed to be at a loss, seems to stimulate a rather superfluous flow of saliva which washed between his phrases, and, when he forgot to swallow, trickled from the corner of his mouth.

He opened an abrupt conversation concerning hypnotism, which devel-

---

[9] Those could be the ruins of the Sugar Mill, since they pitched camp a half mile southwest of it. Ibid., p. 32

oped into a conversation of snake-hunting, to which sport he himself was addicted. He boasted of some such powers as some of the Hindoos [*sic*] profess. This discussion soon digressed into a fuller detail of his psychological prowess. He finished his uncanny discourse by confiding one of his phenomenal powers which he usually kept secret. He said that by a simple act of will he could make his body immune to pain, make his nerves unconscious to feeling. There was an opportunity to call his hand, and you may know that we did. You ask for a practical illustration. He willingly submitted himself to any torture we wished to perpetrate, so, a box of matches being at hand, we subjected him to the "fiery ordeal." We held his hand in the flame of two matches until the matches were entirely consumed. I was satisfied with a quick touch and a quick reflex. But he kept his hand in the flame, laughingly saying that it would not even burn the flesh. When his digits were thoroughly smoked, he rubbed the smoke therefrom to prove that they were free from blisters. We found about three, which he claimed were callouses and, to prove his issue, tore the skin from one, baring the naked quick. He didn't stop there, he started to claw at that too, saying that he could go to the bone without any reaction. We prevailed upon him to quit; we believed him. We were glad indeed to see him go, for he was certainly an uncanny wretch.

Perhaps you wonder why I am writing such a morbid tale, but I can think of little neutral material of interest to tell you, and besides, I want to tell you of the biggest fool I ever met in my life.

I never felt better than [I] do now, I am not working too hard, and I am getting even more experience... *(Letter ends here.)*

September 7: Company D was moved to a point just east of Hamel, near Tincourt, in order to supply "the force necessary" to take over the Roisel–St. Emilie and the Hamel–Heudecourt lines, otherwise known as the CY lines. There were three branch railroad lines. Company D was assigned the CY lines [10] *(Hamel–Heudecourt line) and worked from Tincourt Camp. By the end of September, the regiment operated 39 miles of track—maintained 20 miles, had graded 2 miles, and had ballasted 2.25 miles of old and new track.* [11]

---

[10] Ibid., p. 41

[11] Ibid., p. 42

In France
September 15, 1917

Dear Folks: The last few days have been blue and sunny, but today the gray scud is flying low, and the fields are mournful and misty. A rain here converts the ordinarily beautiful outlook to the dreariest landscape imaginable. In fair weather even the wrecked villages have an aura of quaint beauty about them, but clouds hang over them like a pall, and in the gray haze they assume a wretched and pathetic aspect.

The other day I saw the ruins of a once stately castle. It appeared to be an antique structure with far reaching walls, moss grown and age stained. The yards and parks around it were still beautiful; the blue shaded grass was luxuriant and rich, and deep green where the sun flecked in through the rare chinks in the purple gloom of the heavy foliage above. The trees were giant, and presented a thickly woven barrier of leaves and boughs along the white rock road outside the mansion's yards. The trunks were hidden by an ancient gray wall, but when one entered the park, he could see cruel incisions in the bark of them, made by the Germans before their retreat. Fortunately the British have saved many of the trees, and only occasionally is the perfect blend of the many leaves marred by the white-streaked barren boughs or dry brown foliage.

In the yard stood the skeleton of a hot-house with only a few jagged fragments of glass left in the framework. The rare hedges were unkempt, and had grown awry. Here and there, half hidden in a confusion of tangled wild weed and thistles, the caved entrance of a wine cellar – dark, dank, and musty, perhaps – was visible. Several cellars had been unroofed by a shell, and the rains had transformed them into a reservoir of stagnant water. In several places through the park, the traces of a vineyard might be discovered. A crude implement nearby, which I took to be a wine-press, verified my suspicions.

The castle itself was Destruction symbolized. So complete was the ruin that it would have been almost impossible to restore it or even ascertain the plan of architecture. Not a wall was left as a monument to the structure – all were razed. A castle it was, but now it is a blot of debris, a conglomeration of splintered spars, shards of stone, broken brick, and shattered tile. Red poppies bloom at the edges of yellow pools fringed with green scum and the flies hum their monotonous music there. A black cat slinks among the beams in the evening, and ghoulish rats run riot there at night.

So much for the castle – I shall assume that you are writing, although I am getting nothing to substantiate my assumption. I had a letter from Miss Boggess the other day, and you may know that I was glad to get it. I would like to hear from Clarence, or at least get his address in France if he is here.

I suppose K. and G. are fighting their books at school. France might feel less lonely if I had some missives from some one to peruse occasionally; or some of that romantic stuff the Duchess K. is wont to perpetrate might add a zest to this life. Kathleen had better keep her hand at the pen, for methinks she has a literary sparkle in her phrases. (I really mean that, though I am no judge.) Speaking of school, the school (Ecole Communale) has been open some time here, chiefly at the roof, I think, and in some places in the walls.

Let's have a letter from papa, too, and the school ma'am.

With due apologies for those letters which I have not written, and for those which I have written, I must give my love to all, and my respects to the world in general, and put a throttle on the pencil –

I am, 15 lbs. heavier, Hubert

Sometime during the fall, HWK wrote the poem, "Road to Roisel."

Road to Roisel
Published in the *New York Herald*, winter 1918
Written September–December 1917

I have heard that gipsies dwell
Down the road to fair Roisel.
Tell me true, is this the way?
Surely I have gone astray.

I have heard that gipsy song
Rings the happy way along.
This is not the road, I know.
Why should they have told me so?

I have heard that magpies flew
Black and white in skies of blue.
Surely this is not the way;
Ravens wing the dismal gray.

I have heard the fields were all
Flowered as a gipsy shawl.

This is not the road they mean;
Not a blossom have I seen.

I have often heard them tell
Of the road to fair Roisel.
Nothing did they say, I know,
Of these crosses row on row.

Who has strung that tangled wire,
Blackened hedge and tree with fire?
Is it thunder that I hear?
This is not the road I fear.

Not a thrill of laughter gay;
Surely this is not the way.
Tangled hedge and crumbled wall;
This not the way at all.

There is not a gipsy throng,
Ne're a strain from gipsy song;
Only ranks of marching men.
I must turn me back again.

France
September. 19, 1917

Dear Mother: After I received your letter telling me that you had my letter
from England, I regained the inclination to write, it having left me for a few
days. I was glad to hear from Papa, too, and Grace. I am sorry you put off writing so long. You do not realize how it delays the mail. However, I do not let my
anxiety exceed my endurance. I shall soon get some mail from England, as my
pal got a commission as second lieutenant and went back to "Blighty." Do not
be surprised if you should hear from him. He intends to send me a belt of corp
badges from London as soon as he gets the opportunity.

That reminds me of the souvenir mania with which every one is infected.
Every shire in England has a different insignia for its representative regiments.
The boys here sacrifice an infinite number of francs for these trifles. For a while

the British were selling trinkets taken from the bodies of dead German soldiers, but the graft was soon abandoned as Yankees soon grow wary. German belts must have "Gott mitt Uns" [*sic*] on the buckle, or they have no value; a German watch must have "Hans" engraved on the case, or German hands on its face, or it is eyed with suspicion. (This is unintentional, of course.) For a few days aluminum rings (made from the nose of German Shells) were being sold at five and ten francs, but since we have been to the city we know street venders peddle them there for one franc, 50 centimes. I have limited my collection to a set of English buttons, a German egg-bomb, which was taken from the kit of a dead English Captain, and an insignia which belonged to Ben Holmes who is now in the hospital with an attack of rheumatic fever which he acquired.

We have a "cinema" near here located at the edge of a village. It is in a spacious adobe barn which was spared unintentionally by German shells. The admission for dogs and buck-privates is one half franc, for officers a franc; consequently there are very few officers attending. The show is conducted in a very orderly manner, as the English are very conservative. A barn full of soldiers may well get delirious, however, when the star implants a kiss on the red cherry cheek of the heroine. It is certainly incongruous to see Charlie Chaplin cut his capers and hear the guns roaring at the front while the "Tommies" and "Sammies" howl with laughter.

I was sorry indeed to hear of Ben's misfortune, and Clarence's good fortune. The latter is selfish though, for I was in hopes Clarence would get to France. I was mightily pleased to learn of his success. So Uncle Hamp is a good commissioner for Arkansas? Glad to hear that. Tell Papa that incoming mail is not censored – only the outgoing is criticized.

Give my love to the world in general, and my respects to the remainder. I am your son, Hubert.

France
October 2, 1917
My dear little sister: This is a rather inopportune time to reply to your dainty blue missive as it is eight-thirty and lantern light. This is rather crude stationery too, but I know you will pardon all lack of formality. You don't expect gilt edge and purple ink from France, do you? As soon as I go back to the city *(Amiens, perhaps?)* with a pocket full of francs, though, I mean to send you something even daintier than your sky-blue stationery. When I was there a week ago, I could have bought and sent you a Parisian handkerchief with real French

embroidery around the edges but pecuniary conditions rendered it impossible. After I had indulged in a sad variety of delicacies, bought the requisite apparel, and tipped the beggars at the cathedral, I had only one franc to grace my purse, and consequently I did not mail any silk and linen. Just wait though, and I'll send Paris home.

Perhaps you will be interested to know something of the kiddies in France and England. I haven't seen very many of them. One can't become intimate with scenery, much less the people, while he is riding the troop train. When I was in England I saw hundreds of little Belgians in blue gingham and overalls. Some of them could hardly speak English. They could ask for ha'p'nies though. The English girls wear socks and cultivate as chubby knees as the Highlands ever saw. Another remarkable feature is their red-blob cheeks. I don't know whether it is the climate or the innate red blood of the British that ripens those cheeks, but they are certainly flushed.

These bright-eyed little French lassies take my eye. The buxom, red cheeked English girls are very well, but for brunette graces and dimples, these petite demoiselles for France surpass even some Americans. Of course I am speaking of the little girls. The French boys wear frocks, socks, double-peaked caps, and smoke cigarettes. Little tots who can't even speak bon French trot around after their big sisters with a life size cigarette between their infant lips.

Bon nui ma cher [*sic*]. Taps is about to blow, and I must leave.

By the way, if it is possible will you send me Alan Seeger's poems? It is very hard to get any thing to read here. I resurrected O. Henry's "Options" from the ash can, and have devoured most of it. I would like something heavier. With love, Hubert

Fragment letter to Connie, Hubert's older sister, on the occasion of her engagement to Maurice Hoare:

I have almost forgotten which finger it is since I came here. One doesn't need to know in France. Congratulations, anyway! I am proud of you. There isn't a better lad on the face of the earth than Maurice. Both of you have made a "topping" choice, if you will permit me to quote from our mutual friend the much demeaned Mr. Atkins.

You need not address me as "Bugler" anymore. I am now "Pte" private. The change is in my favor for I have some degree of intelligence – the draft army boys for instance, I mean this. If it is not explicit write me for details. I enjoy your letters keenly.

With love Hubert

Official seal of "night writers" 9:20 P.M. Souvenir of France candle grease *(smudge mark)*

In October, the regiment worked on the Cambrai–St. Quentin railway line on the British Third Army front. Work had to be done at night.[12] Preparations began for the Cambrai offensive. When the 12th began to move army materiel of any description—ammunition, barbed wire, duck boards—from Roisel, Tincourt, and Fins to the front in Picardy, it no longer was called "the quiet sector." It was cold and rainy; work was done at night and camouflaged during the daylight hours.[13]

On October 21, a baseball game was organized with two teams drawn from the seven companies of the 12th. They played eleven innings, often interrupted by Boche planes, and the game was ended by darkness with a score of 1–1.[14]

Sometime in the fall, HWK also wrote this poem about Cambrai:

Cambric

Published in the *New York Herald*, winter 1918

'Tis strange—it was not long ago
I sat and watched my mother sew,
And heard the drowsy hum and whir
Of wheel that flew in gleaming blur;
And sometimes busy scissors snipped
As seams were sewn or seams were ripped.

I often raised a dreamy look
Above my open story-book,
And while she worked her agile hands
My mother told me of the lands
Where cloths were made. I hear her say,
"This cambric came from far Cambrai."

---

[12]Ibid., p. 43.
[13]Ibid., p. 53.
[14]Ibid., p. 48.

It seems as if 'twere yesterday
She spoke of cambric and Cambrai—
The city of the Frankish king
Where looms of magic weave and sing.
That fair old town of northern France
Was but one star in my romance.

The star was not so brilliant then,
But when I see the ranks of men
March past me to the front each day,
I think of cambric and Cambrai;
And every time a cannon booms
I think of Cambrai and her looms.

'Tis strange—it was not long ago
I sat and watched my mother sew,
And heard her tell of far Cambrai,
And now our guns are turned that way.
It hurts me when a cannon booms;
I think of Cambrai and her looms.

~~~~~~

France
October 24, 1917

Dear Folks: A case of procrastination is easily contracted out here, especially in the washing of clothes, the returning of borrowed books, and the writing of letters to those from whom [one] has received no word for a long time. The latter [is] the duty I have neglected, and I apologize with no compunction of conscience whatsoever. Tomorrow, according to rumor we have to have several sacks of mail, and I suppose I shall receive my share, and shall be stimulated to immediate reply.

In my last letter I told you I was a private and a clerk in the company canteen. I am a bugler again. Such are the turns of fortune. I should worry!

Today I went down to the ruins of an ancient chapel to practice on the trumpet. I had never been there before, although I was near our camp. The remains of a garden struggle to grow there, and the fruit trees are shattered by shells, and sapped by incisions. In a quiet hedge-fringed corner of the chapel yard the crucifix stands with the inscription, "Dure" above the Master's head. The roses, pale and pink, bloom around the cross though the frost has come.

Sunday I took a hike of ten miles to some famous battle-fields. One can walk for miles in that country, and see nothing but devastation. Even the roads are destroyed and the lorries do not attempt to traverse those parts. I walked for two hours, and did not even see a poilu or a British Tommy.

The trenches there are deep, eight and ten feet some of them, and the fields are honey-combed with shell holes. Every clod of that ground has been turned. Unexploded projectiles lie half-buried in the loose-piled dirt and chalk. French guns with bayonets fixed and pointed to the old frontier are dropped on the other side of the barbed wire entanglements, just as they were thrown by their owners. White crosses stand everywhere. Some bear the name of the fallen but usually an aluminum plate bearing the simple inscription "Allemand Soldat" or "Francois soldat, Inconnu" is all that is left in memory. Sometimes the blue helmet of the French man is placed on the clay of the grave. Hand grenades, often cases of them, litter the bottom of every trench. There is the egg-bomb cast in iron in the indicated shape, and the cruder German grenade which appears to the impressionistic mind to be a tin can tacked lengthwise to a short round stick. The handle is bored out, and contains a wire which, when pulled, explodes the gun cotton in the case.

The trenches are but the alley of great underground cities, where whole battalion[s] of wet, wretched, lice-eaten men are housed. I walked down a communications trench covered with heavy timber, soil, and sand bags. It was an ill-smelling, gnat-infested place. On each side one could see man-made rat holes framed with boards and leading down flights of crumbled steps to utter darkness. One can smell dead men there.

Sugar beets grow wild in these fields. I ate or attempted to eat one the other day. The sweet one gets at first is very pleasing but the throat burns for several hours from the irritating effects of the juice. The meat of the beet is white, very brittle, and tough.

Someone just opened the door, and my candle flickered so that I could scarcely see to write. One author of highly imaginative qualities overcame a similar difficulty the other day when he wrote the following lines to his unsuspecting girl "My candle has gone out, but I can see by the glare of the liquid fire which the Germans are shooting at us." A Canadian who writes and gives carbon copies to as many girls perpetrated a similar offense when he penned, "As I crawled out of the trench to go over the top, a fifteen inch shell struck me on the steel head but fortunately it was a 'dud' and it didn't explode."

It's getting late and censor is swearing so write often – With love, Hubert W. Kelley.

PS Pardon the signature but it must be written in full.

Work intensified for the 11th and 12th Engineers during the first week in November. Until now, many soldiers had felt let down. "Being first at the front was not the grand adventure we had thought it would be." As one rhymester put it:

> *'Twas to get the Kaiser*
> *that we came to France.*
> *But all we do is to gandy dance!*

But suddenly they were swamped with work. The 11th spent every night from dusk to dawn laying the roadbed for seven miles of track just back of the front line—which they had to camouflage every morning before enemy observation balloons were up. Train crews of the 12th, aided by ground mists, worked 15 to 18 hours a night hauling reserves of ammunition, barbed wire, and rations to the front.[15]

In France
November 1, 1917

Dear Folks: I am overwhelmed with mail. If I showed any impatience in my letters heretofore, it was unjustified, and I apologize. I received a letter from Connie (Oct. 1), one from Mama (Oct. 3) which contained Ouida's and Clarence's latest, and one from the Duchess Katrina (Sept. 26) which contained a friendly little epistle from A.M. together with several cubic centimeters of hot air. As yet I have received none of the parcels but I am waiting expectantly. We have heard that there are an infinite number of loaded mailsacks somewhere in France, and I suppose the packages will be somewhere in the bottom of one of them.

Tell A.M. Frank Lucas and H. Smith that I will write to them very shortly. I have wanted to write to Clarence and Ouida but have not done so since I did not know their addresses. Dr. Marshall wrote me a letter which I received yesterday. Mooney has written me three letters which I have as yet unanswered. So much for the mail.

I went to X___ *(Amiens?)* the other day, and while there I had occasion,

---

[15]Clarence Woodbury, "They Fought with Picks and Shovels," American Legion Magazine, March 1959, p. 34.

as all soldiers who live on "bully-beef" have, to order dinner. The waitress did not appear to have any knowledge of English and I therefore waxed bold and perpetrated a French phrase, "Café au lait," I said very nonchalantly. I interpreted her expression of amusement as an interrogation, and added "Compre Mademoiselle?" Her merriment she manifested as a broad grin. "Yes, I compre. Do you compre that, kid?" I grinned idiotically, and admitted that I did. The mob roared, and I drowned my mortification in the forth-coming thimble full of chicory.

On returning from that unfortunate trip, I caught a lorry at the station to my place of residence. After rumbling over miles of moonlit roads through fields and wrecked villages, the Tommy with whom we rode came to the startling conclusion that the driver was returning over a different road than the one by which he came. We, for I had a companion in distress, alighted without discussing the misfortune. We looked around us and saw the typical French village – a weird spectacle in the moonlight. We asked several Tommies where Y— was, and they shrugged their shoulders, laughed outrageously, and said "Somewhere in France." We walked in circles the rest of the night. We had no gas masks with us, and did not know how near we were to the trenches. We followed every instruction we could gain from camps along the way, and consequently we walked over many roads twice. At sometime in France we came upon a Canadian beer canteen in its last gurgles. The patrons of the bar, who were Americans, some from the States, begged us, after their intoxicated fashion, to spend the night with them but, being unable to prevail upon us, directed us out of sight. We visited five villages that night, some of them twice, and arrived home in the last stages of acute exhaustion. Hereafter I shall leave lorries alone unless I and the driver are absolutely certain of our destinations.

I am so glad that Kathleen is doing well in French. As soon as she is more advanced, I will send her some French books. "Les Miserables," or any of Hugo are available, Alexander Dumas can be bought for two or three francs, and I can get less complicated compositions easily. If there is anything she wants just let me know. Of course Grace is doing well. She couldn't do otherwise.

I forgot to mention that I received a circulating room full of "Stars." I was surprised to read that Lieutenant Maurice Stevenson had landed in France. I may send for my "Webster" pin yet.

I must read some "Stars" before taps so –"Au Revoir." I think I shall absorb some "Jane Eyre" tonight too. I bought it for 1.25 fr when I was in town. I must get up at twelve-thirty tonight to walk guard eight hours straight. I have done that every night this week, but I don't mind a little thing like that—

Good night, with love Hubert W. Kelley

PS If you have received an allotment for Aug.–Sept. and Oct. let me know. I am send[ing] twenty dollars a month. In ten months I shall own a liberty bond, for I am paying five dollars a month for one. It will be sent to Papa.

Amiens became a destination for men on leave. The city, flourishing since 400 AD, was the site of the Notre Dame of Amiens, "the Parthenon of Gothic architecture," according to Viollet-le-Duc. It became a meaningful destination for my father, and he wrote about it in the later letters. He wrote of it again in 1931 and the bittersweet memories it held for him. [16]

As for communicating in French with the locals, most of the men in the 12th never got beyond "Volulez-vous promenade avec moi?," "Combien?," "Oeufs," "Beaucoup," "Couche," "Tres bien," and "Vin Blanc." [17] *Hubert threatened to learn the language during his years there, but wartime did not provide much opportunity for this.*

France
November 4, 1917

Dear Clarence, I am so glad to hear of your success in the medical corps. You are more fortunate than I am. I am classified as a bugler, but I blow only occasional blasts. The rest of my military career is devoted to guard duty, fatigue, and dodging. Of course the education I am getting will be invaluable in the work I mean to pursue. I would prefer a livelier lot than I have drawn, but it must do. If you come to France bring everything the capacity of your kit-bag will allow of, that is in the way of necessities. You will need them. I regret that I did not bring some few things for they cannot be obtained here.

I have been hearing from home every two or three weeks, and so home sickness is plucked ere it has time to mature. *(End of letter.)*

France
November 8, 1917

Dear Mother: Having successfully concealed my bunk from the ever-

---

[16] "A Memory of Amiens," *Kansas City Star*, Sunday, March 29, 1931.
[17] Laird, *History of the Twelfth*, p. 45.

watchful eye of the first sergeant by means of my overcoat and several other members of my ward-robe, which, incidentally are excellent camouflage, I have lit my candle, braced my back against my trunk (which bears the telltale label, "Huntley and Palmer Biscuits") and have entered upon another chapter of correspondence.

I received the parcel of necessities, including the spearmint and cough drops. The latter were very satisfactory despite their medicinal taste. I and my next door neighbor ate them with amazing rapidity and have thus made ourselves immune to coughs till the next shipment of supplies. I was delighted with the handkerchieves, and especially those with the sky-blue effect. I was seriously considering buying another handkerchief but, fortunately you saved me the franc. As for the socks, they are excellent, even more so, since I have observed the price mark upon them. You should see these English socks. They are as thick as puttees, and are the only thing to be used comfortably in these British Brogans. I am still looking for the candy.

This morning early I was sawing some board lengths to be used for bunks when I was told to don my nicest shoes, and my gas mask, and prepare to accompany the Captain to the front. That was the least expected thing which could have happened to me at that moment and the most palatable I could think of.

Unfortunately we did not go as near the line as I wished we might have gone. We walked most of the way under the observation of Fritz who was sitting in his observation balloon at the head of the valley. We walked – for lorries and locomotives are not permitted to come near the line in broad day-light. We passed the reserve trenches, and stopped at the base of a ridge on which is situated an antique bulwark built in the days of Caesar's conquests in Gaul. If we had gone to the top of that ridge the snipers would have picked us off with their bullets. Therefore we stayed at the bottom.

(I just left the hut to see Jerry's fireworks. He seems to have a grudge at the little slope across the field, for he threw three thunderbolts at it just now.)

While I was up the line I saw a lively air battle -- four planes being involved.

I did not tell you that I visited the battle field on which Alan Seeger was killed, did I?

(American poet Alan Seeger was killed at the age of 28 in 1915 during WW I in the Somme, Picardy, France. He was a member of the French Foreign Legion and admired by HWK. "At midnight in some flaming town" is a lyric from Seeger's famous poem, "I have a rendezvous with death.")

Kathleen, you asked for the name of some lonesome soldier who would appreciate a letter. To be candid there are very few here to whom I would have you write. Those who are worthwhile are of good families and are very well supplied with mail. I can tell you of one lonesome Sammy who would like a letter, French or otherwise, very often. His name is HWK. I will keep an eye open though and see. Do not take this as criticism, for it is not; I know your motives are as innocent, sweet, and patriotic [as] they could be, but your letters would be more appreciated by someone with… *(Letter ends here.)*

(Stationery from YMCA headed with the British Expeditionary Force)
November 5, 1917
Dear Ouida: The folks sent me one of your letters, which I received three days ago. I inferred from the epistle that you had been neglected, and that you wanted more mail. I therefore write, because no one realizes that he has been negligent more than I.

I am glad Fidell has done so well in his business. (Fidell Hitchner was Ouida's husband.) Men like him can't very well do otherwise, though. I suppose American Fork is crawling with Fords since he has taken over the agency. We occasionally are in a Ford on these rock roads here. The American Ambulance Corps are using them in preference to heavy cars as their lightweight enables them to traverse mucky roads and perilous slopes.

Nov. 7, 1917 Pardon the intermission, will you, sis? I've been interrupted several times by inconsiderate N.C.O.'s who absolutely refuse to let a man take life easy in the army. Then I just had to swim up the hill to the "cinema" to night to see the pictures, which are shown in a spacious French barn much the worse for shrapnel. Even now my "bunkie" is attempting to snore the candle out so that I may not write.

Do you remember Maren Newby who graduated from Central in 1909? Isn't that the class you finished with? She was Editor of the Luminary I believe. Her younger brother is a pal of mine. He bunks across the aisle (a matter of twelve inches) from me. He is certainly a fine chap. *(Fred M. Newby)*

How is Jr. now? I should enjoy seeing him. Tell him the hop-toads out here are khaki colored, at least some of them have assumed that color. This is true as gospel. The grass in the fields is wet with dew on warm nights and in the morning long, red, slimy, leathery snails are to be found out there. This is a species that Farmer Brown's boy has not yet added to his menagerie. Let us hope that he

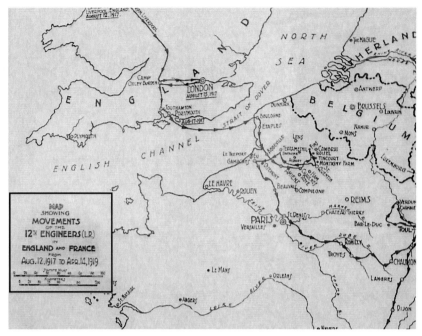

Map of the 12th Engineers Movements in France

doesn't have the opportunity until the war is over. Jr. will soon be old enough to go to school, won't he?

Well, Ouida, good-night and write me often, both of you. I will write soon next time. I'll make it more interesting if possible. I am too sleepy to think clearly. With love, Hubert

During November, preparations for the Cambrai offensive contin-ued, particularly between November 15 and 20. Tanks were brought into broad-gauge railheads, unloaded and taken to nearby camou-flaged positions as concentration points. The roads were jammed ev-ery night with the traffic of heavy guns, light guns, cavalry, wagons, and motor transport. The working radius of locomotives was extend-ed, and men and officers were working 15 to 18 hours per day. The few civilians in the area, elderly men and women, moved in a sad proces-sion behind the lines. The night before the offensive, November 19, was reserved for movement of the supporting infantry. According to one commanding officer, the uncanny quiet that settled over the sector that night was oppressive. [18]

Tanks had been introduced to warfare by the British more than a year before but used in such small numbers that they were not highly effective. But now there were more than 400 of an improved model called the Mark IV. At the first stage, the offensive was amazingly successful. [19]

Sunday, November 18, 1917

(Scribbled in record time Copyright – not to be circulated), France

Dear Folks: Dick Dunn tells me that his wife intimates that I have been very negligent in writing home. No one there has told me that. I have tried to write every two or three days. At least I have written twice a week ever since I have been in France. I shall try to write more frequently, but I shall have to limit my remarks. Life becomes rather prosaic here at times, and consequently one finds a dearth of news.

I have just been over to the barber shop – a very improvised affair with a very improvised barber. A poncho, a towel covered with a veritable camouflage of stains, a petrol can full of hot water, and an assortment of French talcum, German and British issue razors, and soaps from London and Birmingham constitute the equipment. I was relieved of an annoying fringe of foliage around my cranium for the small sum of cinquant centimes. Cheap, eh? While the barber sheared, I heard a rather edifying discussion of the "Latter Day Saints," and a long discourse on "internal fire and brimstone." The author of this brilliant phrase mu[st] have been alluding to champagne or vin rouge... *(Letter ends.)*

At 6:30 a.m., zero hour, on November 19, every battery from Fins to Vermand opened fire—the battle was on. Almost five hundred tanks preceded the first infantry waves. The tanks rolled over the barbed wire and the enemy line was broken on a 20-mile front and to a depth of almost 6 miles. 10,000 prisoners were taken on the first day. [20] *See also Wikipedia and* The Battle of Cambrai, *by Bryan Cooper, 1968, Stein and Day, New York.*

---

[18] Ibid., pp. 55–56.

[19] Clarence Woodbury, "They Fought with Picks and Shovels," *American Legion Magazine*, March 1959, p. 43.

[20] Ibid., p. 56.

France
November 23, 1917

Dear Mother: We have seen some of the more serious side of war the last few days. As I may have mentioned previously, something seemed to be in the air, and my prescience has not proved faulty. The night before the beginning of the "great push" vibrated with activity. The tramping cadence of steel-shod boots on the rockroads – the rumble of lorries – the flashing of many search-lights in the vague mist of the night bespoke a coming storm. Then the calm – the morning, gray, cold, and drizzling the dawn came, silent too, it was. Not the clatter of a limby – not the shrill whistle of a train disturbed the silent brooding.

We had eaten – were discussing the probability of a drive, when, without an introductory shot of a big gun or preface of a hammering machine gun – the bombardment broke in all its awful, rumbling detonation. The push was on. I went outside in the hope of seeing a reflected flash, and was rewarded by see-ing not only the sheet lightning on the distant gray, but the shrapnel bursting in vivid, instantaneous flashes over the trees. Red, white, and green signals flared above the horizon at scarcely perceptible intervals – almost continuously. Air craft, indistinct and hazy in the mists even though they were flying at a stone's throw from the earth at times, glided out of the dim distances like grim spec-tres, and their monotonous hum sang above the thunder in waves as the wind brought the vibrations. But soon the whir of propellers blended with the rush of wings, for flocks of birds, stretching in long wavering lines across the sky, swept over us. They seemed frantic as they sped – they knew not where they flew, they only sought to escape destruction – and it was rampant at the front.

Then came the aftermath, I had seen the troops march up the day before – a solid khaki wall of sturdy Britishers. I saw them coming back the next day in jerky little rattling cars, over an unsteady track. Brave, forbearing lads they seemed – white and mud-stained – but firm in their proud fortitude. One boy held out the bloody bandaged stumps of his arms as the train came by. I was working on the track and I had an unusually good opportunity to observe every train and its contents. Some few wounded Germans were among the British, but they were ostracized in some corner. I was sorry to learn that they were handled harshly by some who could not distinguish between the Prussian policy and the people.

Some few thousands of prisoners passed near here recently, and as far as I [was] able to learn from hearsay, they were an emaciated, dwarfed, and crippled multitude, composed of boys and gray-beards. I realize that the report is exagger-ated, although the more quiet sectors were held by deficients.

The dead still [lie] on the field near us, and are to be seen if one wishes to satisfy his morbidity. One young Irishman was on the field up there for three days watching the body of his brother who fell at his side in the charge. He is heartbroken but is to be given a short leave that he may shake off the horror and recuperate.

You people back there have more sympathy with these things than we. Even though a soldier does not go into the charge – whether he goes over the top or no, he loses sympathy with the human element in war by association with those who "don't care." So many that he forgets the human elements, and thinks of death as a permanent incapacity and a wound as a temporary disability. After one hears Tommy tell of his comrade falling mud and blood bespattered behind him, of Fritz crying, "Mercy Kamarad" to receive a glittering blade of cold steel for his labor, of the gas at the Somme and the shells at Yprès, he rather loses human sympathy and watches all unemotionally and mechanically.

P.S. I received box No. 3—Glory be—

As ever

Hubert

France

November 26, 1917

Dearest Mother: Nothing of import has occurred in the past few days. At the present moment I am guarding two prisoners in a bomb proof dugout. The vigor of their vin rouge has somewhat subsided, however, and the guard is only a figurehead. The regimental band is being organized and a few pieces are running a blaring scale in this resonant place, and you may "jolly well" know that the "beastly carry-on" interferes with one's correspondence.

With Newby, a young brakeman with whom I have been bunking, I have been touring all of the villages in this vicinity since the poilus have arrived. The roads are blue with French uniforms and rairtaillment [sic] lorries. The Nissan huts have been abandoned by "Tommy," and now they are swarming with the "froggies."

Several nights ago Newby and I set out for a village some eight kilos from here. The town has recently been occupied by les civil, and of course after one has seen nothing but the monotony of Khaki for a month, a baggy pair of gray trousers and a pair of wooden shoes, with civilian coat and cap is a relief. We did not reach our destination till dark, and a cold rain was blowing on a gnawing wind. Not a light did we find in the deserted village street. An old school and a chateau or two were the only intact structures in the village and we could not detect a gleam between the closed shutters. We were disappointed with our trip, when a madam opened the door of an apparently deserted house, and scurried off down the road. We called her, but she wisely ignored strangers and disappeared. We found the Town-Major after a desultory promenade through the highways of the village, and were directed to the next town. After a desolate stroll across a rain-swept moor we found the clustered roofs of B____, a very picturesque little place. It was alive with Frenchmen, and we found one whose ____ way was inspired by hunger, even as ours had become, and we followed him. We took a new road; walked half an hour in silence; and soon were dazed to discover that we had landed in the first found deserted town. But after our friend the poilu led us into a civilian home full of light and warmth, we decided that the town was not as gloomy as the outer darkness would indicate.

We bought a half loaf of bread and some fish together with a bottle of wine for Newby, played some French hysterics [?] on the phonograph, talked pantomime to the family and insinuated sentences with a French word or two, and took our leave. We had one other experience with the poilus that night before we reached our bunks with wet skins. We stepped in a French hut, ostensibly to learn the way home, but in reality to get acquainted. The French were as lost as we pretended to be; they brought forth all of their interpreters, who fell before our fluent English. At last five Poilus took us in hand (we could not resist; we started it) and led us back up the road a half kilo; then called out the English M.P. of whom we innocently inquired the way home. He misdirected us, and we followed the path we knew to be right.

~~~~~~~~

Yesterday we took another trip, more aimless than the other. We had not destination in view this time; we caught an ambulance and rode, and where it stopped we caught a lorry – getting off in a wild area where once the troops had fought. Over the downs we went until we came upon a shattered plot of trees, which we found to be an old German stronghold. In the heart of the woods was a vale – a depression somewhat more than a gull, the rim of which was honey combed with dug-outs and mined with tunnels. A chapel, or rather the fragments of the edifice, stood piled at the edge of the wood, and a deep, uncovered tunnel extended from the vale to the scenes of demolition. The church had been the outpost of snipers who retired from their post by the subterranean passage. At the evacuation of the Germans the chapel had been destroyed, and the tunnel caved. A Crucifix had been overturned and torn from its pedestal at the chapel steps. We ascended a double flight of rustic ladder steps to the top of a fir tree where clung a crow's nest or observation post almost fifty feet from the ground. The little platform swayed like a boat's top mast in a high gale. One could survey the landscape for twenty miles radius easily from the post, and could detect the advance of the enemy or locate batteries with binoculars.

When we returned in the gray and silver twilight, we could see the fringe of fire on the battle line. Such an incongruity was there! Around us was peace, a pale moon, and blue downs. We could see the black crows lazily float or flap over the fields; we scared up convoys of magpies or pheasants from the deep grown grass on the bordering meadows. But all the while the ominous rumble of artillery, the glare of star-shells an[d] glare of guns reminded us of a terrific struggle very near us. When darkness came on we overtook a very talkative Frenchman who told us he had killed two Germans with a Jack-knife which he carried with him. He had cut their throats.

True to our instinct we lost our way and found a French camp. The poilus were overjoyed to see us after we told them we were Americans, and they welcomed us around their camp fire. We asked them for water (fortunately I know enough French to get what I want) and they gave us café. It was delicious, especially after three months of English tea. The cook invited me into his billet and showed me his humble bunk – a pile of straw. I told him we slept on beds, and he was as much astonished as Tommy was when we told him we got five "bob" a day.

We reached home tired and hungry; ate a can of bully beef and "retired," anticipating a night's rest. To make a long story short, I was drafted out at 1 p.m. to guard a _____, I'm in again tonight until one, but happily I'm not exposed as I was last night.

(I wrote to Clarence and Ouida)

My friend Sanderson *(Ethan A. Sanderson from Kansas City, Kansas)* nearly lost his life the other night. He went up to the front to watch the whizbangs explode and to visit German "Kontines" etc., when a shell exploded between him and an English Corporal thirty feet away. The two were about to meet but Tommy Atkins was mustarded out with the front of his head missing. Rather unfortunate, wasn't it??

The noise of howitzers has ceased – the guests departed – and (merci bien) the prisoners asleep. I am done) —

I received Grace's little letter, but probably have not commented on it heretofore. That was certainly a good verse she quoted me. I enjoy those little things very much. I shall write to her very soon.

It is getting colder here all of the time, but we manage to keep warm. I love this country, but the lack of freedom which the army necessitates is almost unbearable. Give my love to all. Remember me to Miss Harriman and Miss Boggess. Your own son, Hubert W. Kelley

(Along the side of the second page:)
family secret. (I meant to buy Christmas presents but I am broke. If they are late (don't worry – they won't be much if there are any) you'll understand.

The morning after – (undated)
Weather – Fair
In quarters after guard
Dear Mother: I received an avalanche of mail, candy, cards, and one miniature library from Miss Harriman. Here is an inventory of my post-office:
Kathleen and you – Oct. 26
Papa   Oct. 16
Kathleen and you   Oct. 16
Clarence   Oct. 16
Miss Boggess   Oct. 16
Mr. Stover   Oct. 20
Ouida   Oct. 2
Charlie Smith   Oct. 24

I had just come in from guard duty when I discovered the mail on my bunk. Some kind-hearted Samuel brought it in for me. I have enough "Stars" on hand to start a little heaven of my own. These letters alone are paradise now.

I am so sorry that you have felt blue about me. Perhaps I should not have fretted over mail so much. You rather aroused my ire, however, when you asked me to write more news, insinuating of course that I am confining my letters to immaterial things. That is very true, but if you will observe that the censor has not...*(next section lost)*.

"Mother" seems to have some solicitude about my warmth. Yes, I am hot-headed as usual, but occasionally I am afflicted with cold feet, especially when Fritz spits fire in this area. But, seriously, I have plenty of clothes – overcoat, heavy winder underwear, and brogans impervious to cold, muck, or nine point two's. I bunk in an "upper berth" with a young fellow of a warm disposition; I have a hay stack under me in a bed-sack, five blankets (including my mate's) over me; and all of the heat which escapes from a Sibley stove (bunsen burner disguised, I think) around me. That ought to be warm enough, oughtn't it? Hungry? No! Never! I have plenty to eat, although I think some of the newspapers in "your country" have written some fictitious bills-of-fare which they attribute to our cooks. The background of our meals is "bully-beef" and hard-tack, but of course such delicacies as rice, soup pudding (?), cheese, jam!, and tea (!!) are painted in occasionally. Then with these boxes from home and jam furnished at our expense, and canteens captured from the Germans we have one glorious round of feasting and merrymaking. If the censor is a truthful man he will reject that last line.

So Kathleen got an E in French? Good work! Keep it up. Though once I got E in "Caesar." You know what happened to me, though. Why doesn't she write me a French letter? I would appreciate it, although I cannot guarantee translation nor reciprocity.

Mama: I wrote you a long letter in a blue envelope the other day. I hope you get it safely. These letters will reach you about Christmas, I suppose, judging by the previous ones. Try to enjoy yourselves without Clarence and me, for if we know that you are happy we'll feel the better for it. When I get a blue letter from home, as Mama's last two were, I feel miserable – more so than I would have felt if she had not written at all. I do not worry – I am enjoying life thoroughly – don't make me worry by fearful admonitions to keep out of the guard-house and front line trenches or by worrying over my lack of mail. I'll get along all (write and) right. (At first a mistake and now a pun.) if you keep up a happy disposition, and light heart—

Your good for nothing son, Hubert

Just received a big package from Dad. It was great. Connie's letter of Oct. 29 came with Grace's of the 27. Everything in good shape.

On November 30, when it seemed that things had returned to some normality with trench warfare resumed, the enemy launched his counteroffensive to neutralize the gains made by the British. Enemy artillery opened up on the British positions, rear areas as well as the front line. Shells fell in both Tincourt and Fins camps. The enemy took back Gouzeaucourt and advanced partway to Fins. Wire communications were destroyed before word of the enemy's progress could reach the Canadian and Americans of the 11th Engineers, and suddenly they came face to face with the gray uniforms of the oncoming Germans and their weapons.[21]

---

[21] Ibid., p.62

Clarence Woodbury, a soldier in Company F of the 12th Engineers, a lifelong friend of Kelley and later a reporter for the New York Daily News, *wrote about this famous battle in "They Fought with Picks and Shovels," published in the* American Legion Magazine *in March 1959. He recounts that the Twelfth was working nearby and got mixed up in the battle though not close enough to fight. The Eleventh had left early in the morning for Gouzeaucourt to work on railroad track, believing that the Germans were seven miles away and that they could work in relative peace. They left their rifles at home and many wore jeans over their uniforms. On the way to the work site, traveling by train, a few men noted that there seemed to be more flashes in the distance but did not worry about them.*

This was the first hand-to-hand combat for American soldiers in WW I. Caught without arms, some scattered but most stayed and fought with whatever tools they had at hand, where possible picking up a fallen British comrade's rifle or getting one from a dead German soldier.

The 11th Engineers suffered greatly in killed, wounded, and captured men. One soldier, Woodbury recounted, was taken behind the lines as a prisoner and first asked whether he had any Bull Durham tobacco on him. At least 80 men were missing that night, many of them among the dead. The battle took place on November 30, 1917.

Kelley wrote "'The American Engineers Who Fought at Cambrai,' dedicated to our Brothers in Arms, The 11th Engineers." He read this poem aloud at several gatherings during his time in France, and it was printed in the Paris edition of Stars and Stripes.

The American Engineers Who Fought at Cambrai

This is a tale for those who cry,
America came when the fight was done;
Of Bloody Cambrai where Americans lay
Beaten and brained by the hand of the Hun.
This is a tale for those who say,
Americans came at the end of the fray;
For Americans fell when the Boche brought hell
    Before Cambrai.

This happened up at Cambrai
    to a corps of pioneers,

The first in France, the first to fight
   of Railway volunteers;
Their only trails were daring rails
   to hear the troops and shell;
Their frontier lay up Cambrai way—
   The Border land of Hell.

They sang and slaved, and day by day
   The gleaming steel crept on;
They worked from early morn 'til eve;
   and some from eve 'til dawn.
And inch by inch they laid the line
   as eastward roared the guns;
For well they knew that Cambrai
   must be taken from the Huns.

The British smashed the German line—
   the Boche struck back again,
But Britain staggered but a step
   before the mass of men
Which swept across the ridges like a shining
   scythe of steel;
And sharp must be the scimitar
   that makes the British reel.

The Pioneers were caught unarmed
   within the cruel curve;
The British line was staggering—
   alas, without reserve.
The pioneers could fight or flee,
   and if they turned and fled,
Why—they were non-combatant—
   and nothing would be said.

But these were men whose honor code
   was not the rules of war;
They did not run because they were
   a non-combatant corps.
They stayed and fought, and well they fought,

and all the world may say
That accents of America
    were in the mad melee.
They fought with stones, they fought with clubs,
    they fought with pick and spades
While hid machine guns burned the air
    with furious tirades.
Though shrapnel burst, and fallen cursed,
    and Taubes whirred over head,
They fought like fiends, and when they fell
    they knew they could have fled.

Many a Boche was found that day
    with head wide open laid
By some resisting Yankee pick
    or blow of Yankee spade.
And faces new were seen behind
    the British bayonet
But he who fell and gave his gun
    had nothing to regret.

Up Cambrai way, on fields swept o'er,
    they lie, the men who fell,
And rough-hewn crosses stand for those
    who lived and died so well.
But in our hearts we hold a shrine
    for them—our Cambrai dead;
We know they stayed and fought for us—
    we know they could have fled.

This is a tale for those that prate
    America came for the victor's feast.
Remember the day when Americans lay
    With bayonets bare, and face to the east.
This is a tale for those who say
    America came at the end of the day;
For Americans bled when they could have fled
        Before Cambrai.

France
December 2, 1917

Dear Folks: I have procrastinated, but my negligence demands no apology. We have had our "wind up" a few days, as "Tommy" says, and have thought little of letters. Fritz took a fancy to our rendezvous and hurled a ton or two into our camp. Fortunately no one was injured, and things have lapsed back into the old monotonous rut. One cannot realize that a situation is serious until it is brought to his doorstep in the shape of red-hot éclat, clots of clay and an assortment of debris. When he stands and sees a few geysers of terra firma rise fifty feet in his front yard, hears the bits of shattered chalk and wood rattle on his "tin-hat," he suddenly becomes overcome with an overwhelming desire to leave and with his gas mask trailing behind him, he makes for the high hills surrounding a little tin-roofed camp somewhere in France!

The shell-holes are objects of curiosity, the steel fragments, rather unshapely for their perilous journey, have been collected, and "Sammy's" pockets are turned into miniature ammunition dumps. Everybody has a different tale to tell in defending his actions under fire, and telling which canteen he was going to when the second shell struck.

During the attack, I had presence of mind enough to observe the effects upon those around me. I confess that I was some what taken aback after several shells struck, that my knees were cold, and my remarks abnormally jocose. While some of our boys were running out of the immediate shell area (the only safe thing to do, unless there are impenetrable dug-outs available), I was greatly steadied to see some British troops marching to the front line while the earth was being gutted by the roadside. Not a man flinched, not a file wavered, not an officer moved aside. Steadily – unflinchingly the formation moved up the road with the possibility of being annihilated in the flash of a second. When one sees just such sights as these, he must say with Kipling, "And Tommy, here's my best respects to you." You may think what you will of Britishers, but you've got to give it to Tommy. You can put him in the trenches and he'll stay there till he rots; you can starve him, you can scold him, but he'll fight like the devil just the same. He is slow, but his indomitable beef is irresistible, and his bayonet chills the firmest line of warm patriots. "Fritz" is a fighter, but he can't bear that cold steel.

I suppose that the "Star"[22] was headed with "Sammy eats Turkey," or some other statement equally impossible. We didn't though. We ate stew – hot stew with an occasional chunk of beef in the grease. Hardtack was the second course, and tea (damn that English tea!!) – (don't be shocked – just a quotation from any red-blooded American) and two halves of pears – which, according to the brilliant Katarina, would make a whole pear, but a decidedly awkward one, since they are halves of different pears, and French pears vary in size.

Say, Connie, I have been guarding "Cora Harris's brother," who has a tendency to stray away from camp. He is funny and quaint as he can be, he is well educated – a graduate of the University of Pennsylvania, but he is a too-frequent imbiber of the forbidden drink. You don't need to advertise this. I thought it might be of interest to you. He has hammered out a little rhyme (The Blue Ox) which he sings in all too frequent intoxicated revelries in the dug-out – "The Blue Ox" is the steed of Bacchus – or in American "a big steed [?]."

"O that ox of blue—
He kicks like a nine-point-two." Etc.

I wish someone would send me a package of insect-killer for body vermin – or some dope to put the lid on graybacks. I am not infested, but some of my dear friends have proved themselves to be inhabited. The man who sleeps under the same blankets with me has recently made a successful drive with coal-oil, I followed his example with a can of prevention, just for the benefit of the doubt, you know. I prefer the dry cure – such as powder of some kind. One of the men here has a bellows sort of a box with which he could spray his clothes with powder. Don't be worried over our unsanitary conditions. Everybody is more or less "chatty" in bloomin' France. We have three changes of underwear, we wash every three weeks without fail, bathe every week whether we need it or not, and still we are annoyed by baby "Boches." Please send the powder – just a little bit for emergency.

We have had no mail of late, because of the drive. I presume we will have some soon. With love, Hubert

(It is well documented that lice infested the clothing and beds of all the soldiers. In "Blow, Bugle, Blow," Kelley recounts a humorous anecdote about being bitten by hog-fleas while sleeping in a barn. He

---

[22] The *Kansas City Star* was the daily paper published in Kansas city, Missouri, and Hubert wrote a sometimes humorous serial piece, "Blow, Bugle, Blow," which was published by the *Star* in 1929. After the war, Kelley became a full-time *Kansas City Star* reporter for over ten years.

tries to stand at attention but it is impossible because they are biting his legs and torso. His Captain tells him, "Police yourself.")

France
December 10, 1917

Dear Kathleen: I received your letter, written on the fourth of November, this evening. As usual I keenly enjoyed the contents of it, and could not resist immediate answer. Your French is very satisfactory, as it has thus far hit within the scope of my small knowledge. I often consider kicking myself for not studying more, but it is task enough to write letters in this meager hut. If I ever have the opportunity to be with the French people, I think I will take a deeper interest in the language.

You mentioned my promise of some present to you from France. It will soon be forthcoming. I have decided to break my allotment for a few months in order to buy necessary insurance and provide myself with more francs. At present I am drawing the paltry sum of forty-five francs a month, and with six dollars insurance every pay (I intend taking ten thousand government insurance) I be broke. I think therefore I shall break my twenty dollar allotment, and resume it in a few months. I am not breaking the allotment on your account.

I am glad to hear of your success at school. You had better watch your Algebra though. You, at least, should pass in that impossible subject. Let it be said that one of our family passed in mathematics the first half of Freshman year. (This is not a lecture – just a space-filler and time killer.)

This has been a rather exciting day for us. The past few days have been cloudy, and consequently there has been little activity in the air. Today, however, the sky cleared and the airplanes claimed the sky. For several hours there were numerous inconsequential attempts made by the enemy to cross our lines, and photograph our positions. We recognize a German machine (Allemand Avion) by the cotton-like puffs of white shrapnel smoke which blooms around it. We have grown to take but a casual interest [in] the petty flights which take place over us, and they have been no object of worry. But this afternoon, as I was standing guard, I heard the whir of a plane, and looked up to see a British observation machine some hundred feet above me. He was making for his aerodrome it seemed. Instinctively I knew he was retreating and looked far behind him to see the pursuer. I was more than astounded to see six German Taubes, so-called from the dove-like curve of their wings, I believe, in easy sight. One gigantic battle plane glided in the center of this convoy of five. One might easily discern the crosses on the bottom of the [nether?] planes of them all. The anti-aircraft guns opened up a barking shower of shrapnel, and the machines were enveloped in the forthcoming haze. One must admire the audacity and daring of those men who guided the machines, though they are enemies. They defied the shells which burst in furious numbers around them until they had gained their objective. Suddenly above the rattle of machine guns and bark of anti-aircraft cannon came the swish of a falling bomb, and the detonation as it burst. Then another, another fell and we saw them burst over the ridge, as the raiding squadron wheeled and soared upward out of shell range.

Of course this example of audacity does not compare with that at Yprès. Some of the Tommies from that front say that Fritz swoops down along the roadways, and sweeps it with his machine guns. He dives upon the cavalry camps and kills the horses with his fire. You know, perhaps, that the machine gun is so timed that its bullets pass between the blades of the revolving propeller. The other day I saw an R.F.C. jump from an observation balloon in a parachute when he perceived the audacious Fritz hovering over the bag.

I have become acquainted with a Hindu sergeant. He speaks excellent English. I give him my issue cigarettes and he in turn gives me the satisfaction of his delightful voice. He rids me of all the old K.C. Stars I have at hand, and devours their contents greedily.

I hope you enjoyed Christmas – all of you. Love to all, Your brother Hubert

December 12, 1917

Dear Mother: Alan Seeger's Poems came today, and I shall have something on which to concentrate for some time to come. Oh the misery of the unoccupied mind! And in such a place as this too! One must be conservative in his thought here. If he has no definite subject to analyze and to ponder on, it is very difficult to limit his thought, and so he wanders down a rambling road of fancies which leads into moody wildernesses and melancholy marshes.

I wrote to Kathleen not long past, and mentioned my intention of breaking my allotment. On second thought I do not know when or whether I shall break it. I shall, however, take out the full offer of government insurance which amounts to ten thousand dollars. It would be an injustice to you and me too if I did not.

I talked to a young Irishman a few days ago. He was a light-hearted lad with eyes like two gray pools, each reflecting a star. His hair was typically black and unkempt as the locks of the wind. He bubbled over with delightful blarney – but a thread of seriousness was woven through the colored fabric of his talk.

The fire of his seriousness kindled his eyes and inflamed his countenance as he spoke. He was brilliant in his speech; he was lovable in spirit.

But he is but one of the many I have seen with the shamrock on their sleeves. I feel a sympathy with them – not through any kinship in blood but from a kinship in spirit. I love the levity and melancholy of them, the laugh and the song and the passing shower.

I saw a corps of Irish go to the trenches once. I shall never forget it. They were packed into the open narrow gauge cars – troop after troop. They laughed in their light hearted way, sang their songs – not lustily nor boisterously – but lightly – a natural lyrical effervescence – and puffed at their cigarettes very nonchalantly. One might think they were out for a day's picnic had they not been bound by their battle harness – that they were out on a holiday excursion instead of short, perilous trip to the trenches where they might live with the moles in their burroughs at night, and stand hip-deep in muck from frosty morn till chilling eve. And as the cars rolled away, the little band of bagpipes played "The Wearing of the Green," and the drums rolled like musketry and beat like willing hearts on some remembered field in Erin.

+   +   +   +   +

I saw another thrilling battle in the air. Whatever we may say of the Boche, we must laud his daring and iron courage. Again today my reliable instinct told me something was about to happen. (Now that sounds foolish, doesn't it? But somehow I do feel the proximity of a crisis.) The clouds had broken and blown away, and, though the aftermath of haze still lingered, the observation balloon on the hill ascended. It attained an unusual altitude, tugged at its cables, and finally quieted down like a tired horse, and we forgot it. Later in the afternoon (I was on guard) I glanced at the balloon intuitively, to see several British air planes darting frantically and helplessly around the bag. Then down swooped the German plane. The aviator disregarded everything – he dived headlong for the great bag of the balloon. Then came the rapid angry put-put-put of a machine gun – the bag lurched – wrinkled and burst into a sickening red flame – which grew in volume until a furious inferno dropped through a cloud of black smoke. And high above the smoldering disaster, a Taube circled and sailed away. Slowly-slowly sank two white parachutes sank [*sic*], bearing the observers safely to earth. They had cut themselves loose as Fritz turned his machine gun upon the balloon.

+   +   +   +   +

Near the line, so an engineer tells me, a bursting shrapnel shell shattered the German machine and brought it whistling to earth.

Your own son, Hubert

In mid-December, the first snow fell and stayed on the ground a month. It grew much colder and each man's allotment of 1½ pounds of coal was not enough. Salvaged wood was used to supplement the coal. They spent time clearing the railroad lines, and roads were impassible because of drifting. [23]

The Italian front collapsed and the disintegration of Russia enabled the enemy to move many of his eastern troops into France. Intelligence from captured prisoners confirmed the rumor that the western front was being materially strengthened in preparation for a spring offensive contemplated by the enemy. Toward the end of December, it was reported that the Germans had one whole division for every British brigade in the line on the Somme front. Extended-order drill and target practice occupied the time of troops that could be spared from railroad duty.

Working conditions became increasingly difficult due to enemy bombing raids and artillery fire that wrecked track and equipment. Army orders required the construction of an earth or chalk wall 3 to 4 feet high and 2 feet thick around each hut or tent so that a direct hit on any hut would be localized by the protection. [24]

December 16, 1917
Amiens, Somme
France

Dearest Mother: I came here last night for a brief breathing space of twenty-four hours. It is only rarely that we have the opportunity of visiting civilian cities untouched by the blighting hand of the Boche.

I am writing in a home like little café where the air is warm and heavy, hazy with blue smoke, and laden with the appetizing odor of French fried potatoes, steaks broiled, and eggs. This is indeed a relief from the coarse milieu to which I have become accustomed. There is a dainty mademoiselle serving us, and it goes without saying that it is quite thrilling and blushingly disconcerting to have her put her hands on your temples or her arms affectionately on your shoulders as she awaits your order. At any rate, it is an experience. Of course, you must understand that I am not impressed by her amorous approaches; I am

---

[23] Laird, *History of the Twelfth*, p. 71.
[24] Ibid., p. 73.

well-educated enough in the ways of the world and of France to know that my juvenile appearance is apt to be trifled with. This is a pathetic fallacy but you will understand.

This city is very cosmopolitan. The streets are thronged with natives of the four corners of the earth – Hindu, Algerians, Scotch Highlander with kilties aswing and English officers smart with canes atwirl. There are poilers dressed in gaudy braid and blue uniforms. There are chasseurs from the alps, yeoman-like aviators, old grizzled veterans with a clinking assortment of medals – Croix de Guerre, Croix Militaire – and some with the V.C.

The streets are very crooked and narrow – the aisle walks were made for Indians. Vehicles of every description rattle over the cobblestones – the carts of fruit venders – wheel barrows high-piled with merchandise and pushed by some sinewy little woman, dray-carts, wagons, and quaint little four wheeled cabs bearing extravagant Americans happy with champagne. All of the buildings here are low structures of four or five stories, the windows high and the architecture square. Adobe or plaster is used on the façade and this is usually painted in light shades of pink, yellow, or blue, which adds a tone of picturesque beauty to this whole cities [sic].

The Cathedral d'Amiens is one of the most beautiful in France. Notre Dame de Paris – de Beauvais and de Rheims ranking as the others respectively, I think. I may have ventured some details of this magnificent edifice previously. I love to walk its corridors, hear its echoes, or stand silently and awed before some chaste, marble shrine, where these spiritual French come to light quiet flames for "Our Lady."

I only have the day left, so I must cut this short. This is a difficult place in which to write, as these Canadians are loud of temperament.

Well, goodbye, for a while. I am in the best of health, am growing brawny and wise. I will write again soon. Your letters have all been received and it is indeed a pleasure.

With love Hubert

France

December 26, 1917

Dear Mother: I have been on guard most of the week, but Dick Dunn (Corporal of the guard) released me this afternoon, and I shall take the opportunity to write to you. I started a letter yesterday to you but somehow I never finished it.

This morning found me with a brown taste in my mouth and a dissipated feeling in my head, but it will not last long. Yesterday's feasting was too much for us all. After one has become accustomed to army grub, such food will go to his head. We dined on turkey and plum pudding yesterday and it has been too much for us. Yesterday afternoon I got Ouida's package, one from Harlie Smith, and a book of the last "Poems of the Great War" from one Sgt. Major P.E. Mains, 60th Brigade Depot, Ft. Sill, Okla. I don't know him, I'm sure but I am almost afraid to write to him for fear he is a neglected friend and I don't want to hurt his feelings. All our Christmas mail has not come. I am expecting your package in a few days.

Last night we had a program in an improvised theatre made for the occasion. Several boxing matches were staged, one wrestling bout, and a quartette sang. One of the lieutenants insisted that I recite that piece of doggerel ["Ravings of the Rum Hound"], which I did with the customary effect. That piece is rotten, but it seems to touch the spot with these switchmen and engineers, and they appreciate it though repeated. They like the truth of it, I think. Perhaps I shall have some real verse to send you sometime.

Those poems of the war are certainly inspiring. I can doubly appreciate them in the atmosphere of the war itself. One poem is by Charlie Hamilton Sorley, a young Captain – look it up.

"All the hills are vales along
Earth is bursting into song.
And the singers are the chaps
Who are going to die perhaps."

It is crude I think occasionally but it is beautiful. Another verse is by Rupert Brook. He was killed at the Dardanelles.

"There is a corner of some foreign field
That is for ever England."

You know the poem I p_____. One phrase in it I like so much is (not verbatim) "Let my life be a pulse in the eternal mind." *(The line is actually "And think, this heart, all evil shed away, / A pulse in the eternal mind, no less / Gives somewhere back the thoughts by England given...")* That is a noble thought, don't you think. Why don't you get the book; it is great.

We had a white Christmas. Last night the moonlight and the snow made day of darkness. I read a newspaper outdoors to see if it were possible. Today there have been snow flurries and we are almost snow-bound. The sun is shining soon, though, and the thaw is dripping and tonight it will freeze.

Before long we are to be given seven day leaves in France, I think. If I go I shall divide my time between Marseille and Paris. I would like to go to "bonnie Scotland," far in the "Heelands" away from war. I would like "Owld England" but between the impossibility of leaving France and Sinn Fein, I shall be content with having seen her shore. It will be necessary to have beaucoup francs for such an occasion as leave, and if [I] should know certainly that we are to go, I will write for cash. I have not broken my allotment and shall not. I want to think the situation over a bit more.

You must forgive this "beastly" letter, you know. Can you "fawncy" one writing with a dim cold _____ [roindor?] on one side and a poker game on the other—

> The Women's Auxiliary of the 12th Engineers sent supplies and Christmas boxes to the soldiers. Each camp had a Christmas Eve celebration, with Montigny camp having the most unique with a cedar tree and a generator for electric lights. Socks were filled with popcorn and homemade ornaments were decorated. On Christmas Day, the men had bully beef and some turkey brought in by truck from Nevers by a Lt. Johnson.[25]

France
December 29, 1917
Dearest Mother: Our mail has been somewhat delayed by the heavy snows, I suppose, and writing has been somewhat discouraged. Every time we get anything from home, be it letter, card, or parcel, we clog the post with our letters of appreciation etc. etc. Today we received a bag of necessities and comforts from the "Red Cross." Part of it had been sent from Paris, and Parisien packages are not incentive toward home correspondence.

I have another "job" now. It involves much walking, and I have the longed-for opportunity of being away from camp. If there is anything I dislike, it is confinement. Let me be outdoors seeing and doing! I can see much walking from one end of the line to the other, but I do very little. The winds are heavy

---

[25] Ibid., p. 75.

now, the dry snow drifts – it is blown in low streamers on every blast; and travel is rendered very difficult. I enjoy the cold mornings keenly, nevertheless. This morning the full moon was still bright when I left camp. The sun – round and red heaved over a bleak ridge while I was on my way. I quit the railroad track when I reached my destination, and returned on the rock road. The wind was like a whip, the snow sleety and sharp. Two miles of the weather afoot would have involved a pair of well-numbed feet. As I was about to turn to some way side but for warmth until a lorry should pass, I heard a rattle and bump on the frozen road, and turned to see a two-wheeled cart tip over the hill, pushing a skidding donkey before it. I hailed the driver as he passed, and found that we were bound for the same place. Then a flying leap, I landed in a pile of rumpled blankets behind the seat. It was but a second until I had scrambled to a place beside the red whiskered driver, who blew his nails industriously, and spoke not a word. I heard a rustle, glanced back at the blankets, and detected a movement in the folds, which became more vigorous and frantic. Finally two hands emerged from the squirming mass, the opening was farther parted, and a "Tommy" came out, head and shoulders, very startled and sleepy. "And what's the matter," he queried, "Did a bloomin' bomb light me on me head?" Then I realized that I had deliberately hopped on his face when I made my flying leap, and I begged his pardon profusely. He was not enthusiastic about accepting my apology; I left him alone to nurse his bruises; and he crawled back in his blankets. We rode on –

Some of the geniuses in the black smith shop have been printing a daily gazette on the walls of their hut with chalk which is very abundant in this country. Some very interesting tabulations are made. They are very funny to me, although they are not witty always. The seriousness with which the lines stare at you, and the grinning absurdity of their sense, make a comical incongruity. Some of the head-lines read:

An anti aircraft gun brought down a crow twelve thousand feet high today.

Ninety sacks of mail arrived at the headquarters this morning.

Three hundred yeoman [?] girls will be stationed at ___court January first.

After December twentieth all drinkers of rum will be classed as rum-hounds.

This place is "out-of-bounds" for all rum-hounds.

Thanksgiving – Let us be thankful for our bully-beef and tea.

After tomorrow all men who work hard will be given ten days leave in Paris.

All men making good on the football team will be given rum.

These things may seem foolish to you, but considering the circumstances, they are funny. We hear such foolish remarks as those (sometimes more subdued) circulated for the truth.

Well, bon nuit, I want to read a bit before taps. I am still looking for your package (Xmas) but it will come. Half of our mail hasn't come. If Dick's wife calls up tell her he is alright all around. He certainly treats me as if I were one of his own.

Hubert

Letters from 1918

At this point in the life of the Twelfth, loneliness and melancholy set in—it was a desolate country and the winter weather made it worse. Athletic goods, books, magazines, and phonograph records were provided by the YMCA representatives but could not have done very much to relieve life under fire and tension. A recreation tent was put up for Company D, and later a piano was obtained. In January, there were 18,646 locomotive railway miles maintained by the Twelfth.

Seven-day furloughs with two days' travel time began for the men. During his leave, a soldier could go anywhere in France. Major Laird, author of the History of the Twelfth Engineers, assumed command of the Twelfth regiment in January. [26]

France

January 1, 1918

Dearest Mother: I have finished my morning's work and it is yet early in the day. A bitter wind is blowing the fine cutting snow in drifts, and transportation is rendered rather difficult. When the weather is tolerable, I stay out as long as possible, riding the trains or lorries from one gang to the other. When I am

---

[26] Ibid., p. 77–78.

out and away, I can see what is going on, salute the Hindus and hear Tommy complain of the weather, condemn all officers in general, and avow his undying hate of the Boche, France, war, and "bully-beef."

I didn't stay up last night to "smash baggage" for the new comer, but I find that he has arrived this morning. Some of the night men say that guns were fired before and after twelve o'clock, so I assume that the intermission was the reverential silence in honor of "nineteen eighteen." I don't know exactly what to resolve to do this coming war [*sic*, could mean year], if a resolution is necessary. Perhaps a pledge of more frequent correspondence would be appropriate. I keep decent hours perforce, rising by ten minutes of six and crawling in by nine-thirty. I usually have my second shoe off at taps. "My pardner" plays poker to the last minute, and we turn in to-gether. On these winter evenings, one has very little to do. Occasionally I wash my face in the petrol can, or comb my hair. It must be done at least once a day, and the event usually takes place in the evening. Last night some of the boys sang, and the harmony erased a few hours. I have been reading a cheap novel, "Sundown Slim," and it affords some pastime, but it will soon be gone, so I think I shall write more letters. I have written a new rhyme, "The Ravings of a Rum Hound," which I have been asked to perpetrate as a "New Year's Festivity," and which will not be if I can see my way clear. It was written at request for some of the "fallen" brothers, and has been lauded as "being able to get a drink any old time." (*see P. 122*)

Tell the kids to write me; I know Connie will. I got a letter from some British belle at Birmingham Eng. the other day; also I have the address and invitation to write to one very nice Mme Yvonne in Amiens which I shall not do. That English girl writes a delightful letter – very modest, etc. She says, "You may write to me if you like." Her address is very picturesque too. These English addresses are far superior to ours. You don't have "1010 E. 10th" or "Corner of 10th and Main" or some other prosaic and commercial address. You have for example, "Sunset Cottage, Virginia Waterside, Surrey." Or "Yoleshill near Stratford-on-Avon – Twenty-two Crossroads." That's an address worthy to be rhymed. Whoever lives at the first one is not commonplace.

Give my love to everyone – Your son, Hubert

France

January 5, 1918

Dear Dad: I have your letter of the fifth at hand, and I am glad to hear that business is good. I hope you do not feel too uneasy about the articles you read in the newspapers. They seldom get anything straight so far as I am able to ascertain. We were not, as a company, actively engaged in the Cambrai drive, contrary to the statements of the "Star" [the Kansas City Star]. Our camp was shelled about that period but nothing was damaged. My past letters probably have relieved your mind by this time, but I have just learned of the sensation created by a false report.

Dick Dunn's wife was greatly excited by the report, and I suppose Mama felt very great anxiety. I am so sorry that this has occurred.

Dick Dunn certainly thinks the world of you. He speaks of you whenever we talk together at any length of time. He is going to make arrangements for both of us that we may be together on leave if possible. I wish that you would send me forty or fifty dollars if you think it safe. Heretofore I have been getting most of your letters, and I think that you can get an express order across easily. I can cash it in Paris when I go there. It may be some months before I go, but I am sure that I am to go, and I would like to have the money, as what I draw does not amount to very much. I intend taking out insurance by the first of February, and that would reduce my income to two or three dollars a month. That will not see me through Paris prices, and perhaps Marseilles [*sic*]. Let the matter drop if you think it unwise, good. I think I can manage without it.

I have written Clarence a letter since he went to Houston. I hope he does not have to come to France. It would be a great experience for him but—

Marquis has not written me; I should like to hear from him very much. If Wallace is in France, I should like to hear from him, if he is near me. He is in a railway regiment, or he is in the British army or — labor battalion.

With love, your son, Hubert

PS if you think an express order unwise, perhaps you might send a draft on the "Banque de Paris."

France
January 11, 1918
Dearest mother: I have only a few minutes before mess, and shall take this opportunity of letting you know that I am well. Dick Dunn when I last saw him was well, and should his wife call up you may tell her. Nothing of unusual interest has happened here in the past few days; the rain and snow have rendered activity practically impossible. We are still in the same camp [Tincourt]; we have made it comfortable as possible for the winter. We hope to join our own forces in the Spring. I am sick to see American infantrymen marching to the

line, although from another standpoint I should be sicker if I saw them go.

Some of the men who have been to the coast say that they have met drafted men, and that most of them are afraid they will never fight – that the war will soon be over. They need not fear. Revolution in Germany is the only hope for immediate peace, I think. We have heard that twenty-five thousand Austrians refused to come to the Western front after Russia had made her temporary truce. There is no verification for this. I hope it is true — but — (rumor?)

I have been out checking men on the track most of the morning. After I finished I went down to the blacksmith shop and joined a coffee party. They (the Blacksmith and helper) make coffee on the forge (a real treat out here.) We usually have nothing with our mess but blooming tea—

With love, Hubert

The first serious train wreck occurred on January 15 when an engine and train left the track on the Vermand Line near Montigny Sugar Mill. Two British soldiers died and there were minor injuries to eight others. A British officers' inquiry found that the accident was unavoidable due to the inability of the engineer to control the train on the steep grade with slippery rails.[27] On February 1, the regiment came under the A.D.L.R. Fifth Army (south), British. The British colonel was at first skeptical of the Americans but later said that the Twelfth was the most efficient railroad organization he had known during his entire experience with the Allied armies.[28]

France

January17, 1918

Dearest Mother; I have neglected to write for several days, as I have been writing and thinking almost constantly during my spare time. As you may notice by the stationery, I received the Christmas package. Though it was late it was appreciated very much. The knitted cap will be especially useful.

I sent home for fifty dollars for my leave. By the time you receive this I may have sent a cablegram for the money. Dick Dunn and I hope to visit Paris together. As soon as we get the money, we are going.

---

[27] Laird, *History of the Twelfth*, p. 77.
[28] Ibid., p. 78.

As I said before, I have been busy. The New York Herald (Continental) has offered several prizes for verse written by American soldiers. Unfortunately, I have had little inspiration and very poor conditions under which to write. I only had two or three days to complete my manuscripts, and they are not what I wish them. They must do. One thousand francs is offered for the first poem, five hundred for the second, and one hundred for those which are worthy of publication. I am working on some others which I hope to complete before it is too late.

I am enclosing typed copies of those I am sending, and incidentally a written manuscript concerning the ideals of a hungry soldier. I am not submitting it. I will number the poems. Number 1 concerns an old gypsy town ["Road to Roisel"?]

No. 2 An impression of childhood

No. 3 Wine time in Picardy which I have already sent you.

With love, Hubert

Cambrai is pronounced Cambray. Even accent.

Vintage
1918
Or Wine Time in Picardy
Published in the *New York Herald*

Then

'Tis wine-time in Picardy;
The cluster bursts and drips.
  Oh, pluck it ere the sun's caress
  And earth's sweet thirst deny the press
And rob our lips.

'Tis wine-time in Picardy;
The hamlet rings with mirth.
  The casks are drunken with their hold;
  The casks are cooling in the mold
Of burrowed earth.

'Tis wine-time in Picardy;
And lips are purple-wet
  What white-gleamed challenges they pass

Across the crimson-glittered glass,
And eyes are met.

Now

'Tis wine-time in Picardy;
The vines are torn awry.
  The straggling fronts have crept around
  A solitary, sodden mound,
To brown and die.

'Tis wine-time in Picardy,
And homes are razed and wrecked.
  The poppies breath[e] their drowsy breath
  In gardens of decay and death
And long neglect.

'Tis wine-time in Picardy,
But with abundant yield;
  For wine that comes not from the press,
  The earth may drink and we may bless,
Flows on the field.

~~~~~~~~

France
January 22, 1918

Dearest Mother: We have had no mail for so long that there is very little incentive to write. I have been busy working on that competition of which I spoke, and have neglected my correspondence. By th[e] time you get these lines, I suppose the mail [will] have come; in fact, I am not sure but what some mail will come this afternoon.

One of the master engineers has gone to Paris, and Dick Dunn and I are occupying his hut while he is gone. When I finish checking up in the morning, I come here, and clean up, make a fire, cook something for our dinner, and write. Dick usually comes in about eleven thirty, and fries a pan of potatoes, which, by the way, were not issued. We "manage" for them. Fried potatoes are a luxury. I finished making a can of custard out of condensed milk and custard powder. We will have it for dinner. The can is cooking in the window now.

This is a dingy, cramped little hut, but after I have lived in other quarters, I think I would be satisfied here all my life. A man is contented with very little here. (I shall send you a copy of the last verse I wrote, but I have none handy at present. Speaking of the hut reminded me that I have found it easier to write verse here than in the Nessen hut [Nissen hut]. One can accomplish a deuce of a little with a poker game at one hand and a prizefight at the other.

I have been writing to that English girl I mentioned – the one who lives in Birmingham. I shall send you one of her letters. They are excellent. She is only eighteen, but she writes like a woman of experience. She perpetrates such phrases as these: "I have a sister – a most precocious child – in whose society dullness is an impossibility. She subjects our cat to frequent dental examinations, which operations he bears with the utmost fortitude." That's pretty good, I think.

? ! ! ! * (! !— [*sic*]

The aforesaid custard just now was ruined – alas. I had the can cooking in the window above me, and the wind blew the window shut, and the custard dumped over on me, my desk, and my tablet. Dick and I shall go custardless. I just finished cleaning up the lake of custard on the table, and the pool in my lap. Such is life!

With love, Hubert

P.S. Enclosed find a copy of one of the verses I am using for the competition.

Somewhere in France

January 26, 1918

Dearest Mother: Dick Dunn and I are still to-gether. This is our last night, alas, for tomorrow the master engineer returns, and we must evacuate his hut. Then we must go back to the turmoil of the bunk rooms, the poker games, the swearing matches, and the lousy multitude. Paradise comes in short sweet doses here, like cough medicine.

I recovered my French books, and shall resume study. An operator who lives at the last station before the trenches had them, and I went after them, and brought back not only the books, but also a loaf of bread and a can of jam. Rather profitable trip, was it not? Dick and I had a celebration.

Your letters of Dec. 13 and Dec. 29 came with a letter from Miss Boggess, even as you prophesied. Connie's letter of Dec. 17 came in the last mail too. The box which you sent containing the 'goods of questionable character' was received, appreciated, but as yet there has been little occasion for its use. It shall come with the warm days. Thanks!!

You are still begging for me to ask for something. There is nothing that I can think of, outside of a pass to Paris, to ask for, and you could not help me there. I read your letters to Dick Dunn, and he remarked, as I read your appeal for a request from me, that that was "just like a mother."

This is a picturesque little hut. It might be taken for an Apache rendezvous, if some gendarme should come upon it. We might well be taken for Apaches too, with our disheveled hair and grimy countenances.

On the improvised table stands the candle-holder – a green ale bottle. Long white streaks of candle grease plaster the neck which a short soft stub burns with a yellow, smoky flame, at the mouth of the bottle. Cigarettes litter the place; there is an open package on every shelf with fire-stained pipes with ill-smelling bowls, shreds of black tobacco, and burnt matches are strewn about me.

Kansas [C]ity has been unfortunate. It is a shame that she must have to contend with small-pox right at the start of the war. I do hope Kathleen and Grace are well by now. This vaccination problem is serious and the process dangerous. We had to endure it in the States, but we are immune now to both small-pox and typhoid.

Last night was clear and the moon was full. The German raiders take advantage of such a night and make attacks with bombs. Dick and I were making custard when the first attack was made (not on us, of course) but near enough to be heard. Incidentally, we continued to make custard when the machine gun tut-tutted the Gotha [German plane] as it came over with a second load, but a fog made a third attack impossible, and we ate our custard in peace. My motto (likewise Dick's) is "I can't be bothered." A man can't afford to be bothered.

A young fellow just came from an English hospital to join our company a few days ago. This is his first experience in France and he laughs in high glee at all our "winded" remarks concerning shells, hay-rocks [?] and machine guns. "Oh," he says, "Why be afraid? This is not bad." "Listen here," I said, "You'll have your wind up when you learn how. We've been in France five months and you five days."

An English captain once told me that the rookie refused to dodge a shell, take refuge from a bombing raid or carry his gas mask. "That is because he is ignorant," he said. "When men stay here a year or two, they'll dodge when they hear someone whistle Tipperary." That is very soothing; it justifies so much our timidity. We have begun to learn.

I am looking for that last "substantial" package; it should be here pretty soon. I am patient, though, or at least, try to be.

With love – Hubert

France
January 29, 1918

Dearest Father: I received your letter of the twenty-ninth, and thought the verse, "My Town," was very good. The goods of "questionable character" arrived two days ago, as I may have mentioned in a previous letter.

Dick Dunn is still fretting over that letter you haven't written yet. I agree with him that you are too busy, but I know he thinks himself neglected. From the way he talks he writes to you very religiously, and I believe, with him, that you should reciprocate.

I am very glad that Clarence is still near home. I only hope he gets to stay. I know he is anxious to come over here, but he will be as anxious to leave again. It's a great experience but—!!

Dick Dunn and I hope to go to Paris soon. If the fifty dollars I sent for has not come, I shall go anyway, as I can obtain what money I need, with the understanding that it is to be paid back at a later day.

As to that verse. "Wine time in Picardy," if you think it worth while, you may publish it, or, at any rate, attempt it. By the time you receive this, you may have received a better copy of the same verse, along with several other newer ones. I really don't care what you do with them; they are of little consequence. If you think the other one worth while you may publish it.

We witnessed a rather spectacular attack on a Gotha last night. We saw "shrapnel bursting in air" very near our hut, while a nearby machine gun turned a veritable rod of steel bullets on the enemy machine which persistently buzzed above us. The first bullets were tracers – bullets lit with green fire, phosphorescent, I presume, and we could follow their trail from the gun, across our roof, and away. The sight was thrilling in the extreme.

We have been having very clear weather here of late, and air raids are frequent. The weather is pleasant, though at night we suffer from the heavy frosts. The sunrise here is beautiful. The skyline is level and bare, and the effect is not marred by buildings or trees. It is hard to realize, when the sun heaves over the ridge on a world of white frost, that this is a war-ridden country. The aspect is so peaceful.

I must close. As ever, Your Son, Hubert

France

January 31, 1918

Dearest Mother: I will write just a few lines to let you know that I am well. We have been having excellent weather the past few days, but a cold mist envelopes everything this morning. We have been troubled with a full moon every night for the last week. Fritz takes advantage of the clear nights, and drops bombs in the vicinity of this sector. Last night when the poker game was in full swing, and the francs were flowing freely, one of the grizzled gamblers turned to me and said, "Has that damned moon come up yet?"

The box of candy came yesterday very unexpectedly. The upper layer was somewhat the worse for the Halifax explosion or a submarine bombardment but it was edible, and that was enough.

Did I tell you about the tall switchman who made an error worthy of Mrs. Wood B. Highbrow? He was describing a Frenchman of his acquaintance in this manner: "He was a slim sort of froggy with an artistic moustache, and he had one of them there cross due croys hangin on his breast." There are many Frenchmen wearing the "Croix de Guerre" and the owners are highly respected.

I want a good dictionary. I procured a cheap pocket-edition at St. Louis, but it is not exhaustive enough. I want a small, well-defined dictionary that be carried easily in a haver-sack. There is no hurry about sending it. Send one of the extra ones at the house, but do not take it if it is needed. A second-hand book will answer the purpose very well.

Give my love to all, and do not worry about me. I am away at school, and will soon be back. Your Son, Hubert

January 31, 1918

Dearest Connie: I have been receiving letters from you often, but I have not answered them individually. I have tried to make any letter home suffice for all. Of late, I have spent very little time with correspondence. Perhaps I have spent all my energy on the few little verses, which I have been working out, and have not made my letters what they should be. I shall reform.

Miss Sanderson must not think that I have any "inside information" on the war. We have nothing but rumors. Rumors sweep this country like a gas alarm. Gas shells may be concentrated on some point in our sector and a cloud formed. A cloud of gas can be carried in tact on a slow wind for a distance of twenty miles. A gas gong or siren starts the alarm, the next post takes it up, and in several minutes, every camp in a wide area is notified. This is somewhat of a digression, but it is interesting. Gas is a cruel thing – its effects too horrible to describe. We "stood-to" two nights ago with masks at "alert." It was my duty to see that every man in the company was awake, and I was given more than one "cursing" by irritable sleepers who were loath to crawl out of bed. There was little danger, but it is best to prepare. While the gas scare was critical, the Boche dropped bombs at points near here. It was an exciting experience. An air attack at night is very uncommon.

I shall write Glen a personal letter when I receive the box you are sending.

Give my warmest regards to Maurice. I hope he doesn't have to come, but I'm afraid he will not bless me for my wishes.

With love, Hubert

PS Tell Miss Sanderson that we are very ignorant as to the time of peace. We get very little information here, let us hope—!

France
February 10, 1918

Dear Connie: I got another package to-day – the one containing the gum from Glen. I shall enclose a letter to him in this envelope. You people are not getting all my mail, or I am neglecting to receipt all your letters. I try to answer them all, but perhaps I overlook some of the contents. Now I have two photographs of Grace and Kathleen together, and one of Kathleen. I had a letter from Maurice too. That is the mail under question I believe.

I am still waiting for my money. I cannot go on leave until I get it. I am not impatient though I cannot wait indefinitely. I am going to Nice, for Paris is engaged for months ahead (for our company). I wish you could be with me. We would take some real hikes in the Alps, view the old Moorish cities together, and travel the road to Cannes and Cagne.

"and hear the blue sea's booming roar
Along the northern Alpine shore.
Walk hand in hand with fair Romance
Beneath the southern sun of France."
...*Extract from one which is not written.*

I meant to go with Dick Dunn but I am not sure that I should now. I may go alone!

I want to learn to speak French very much. I can make myself understood somewhat even now, and hope to carry on a conversation by the time I return from leave. As I may have said in a previous letter, I had a delightful time with

*Top: Hubert Kelley and
Fred Newby, 1918*

*Bottom: Hubert, WWII
War Correspondent*

Amiens Cathedral

Top: Exterior view

*Bottom: Interior, the
Editor in the foreground*

the Italians some days ago. French can be used in Italy, that is northern Italy. Nice is very close to the Italian border, you know. One of the Italians understood Spanish. If you had been there, you might have explained that we are not accustomed to take donations for the "Bull Durham" [tobacco] we give our comrades in arms. I never did make him understand.

Sanderson and I struck out early in the evening. We were not sure where the billets of the new arrival were. En route to "Little Italy" we took in a cinema and vaudeville show. It was a cheap performance – twenty-five centimes for the gallery, and fifty for the pit. We stood in the gallery; the pit was full. We understood little but enjoyed the bright lights and tinsel. The theatre was an abandoned French barn, but the British had decorated it so effectively, that it might well trump some of the "Empress" patrons, featured in a sketch. He claimed to have worked on a ranch in Massachusetts. The Tommies didn't object though; many of them think that cows are punched in Hoboken.

We waded down a dark road, which had been converted into a river of mud by the snow and heavy traffic (guns) and lorries until we came to a little row of cottages, once destroyed, but now restored for the use of troops. The hanging light of candles slanted to bright squares on the road way gr— the open doors and we could hear the boisterous jargon of foreigners ring from the interior. We entered and found ourselves in a dim room both sides of which were pigeon-holed with bunks. Most of the Italians had retired, but they sat up in bed and welcomed the "American." They were all besser [*blesser means injured in French*], having been wounded on the Piave and were unfit for trench service. Some were handsome men, as fine as I have ever seen. They were anxious to learn, repeating every English word we spoke. They tore the insignias from their collars and presented them to us as souvenirs. I wear one on my hat, but my hat has gone on leave with a comrade.

Yesterday a real "dago" came over to our camp. He carried an American flag in his pocket and spoke English like "Old Joe, the Huckster." He had worked in Des Moines eight years. One of the boys showed him a "five dollar bill" and his eyes lighted up as he stroked it lovingly. He was "fed up" if a man ever was, and said, "If the Germans leava my life alone, I go back to Iowa." He was a good American. "Don't you want to die for your country?" asks one of the cooks. "I die for my country lika hell," answered Frank. "I go back to Des Moines." He need not worry; he'll go to Des Moines when he dies.

I've got to write a little letter to Glen before I get too sleepy, so good-night this time, Connie. I'll write again soon –

With all the love in the world, I am your brother, Hubert

The Battle of the Piave River, June 15–18, 1918, was an important victory for the Italian army and the Allies.

During February, the regiment was increased by 551 men. There was a steady increase in the volume of engineer materiel handled and in personnel movements. Work was not completed, however, and that, combined with the French drawing their left wing south of Vermand, contributed to the results of the terrible Somme defensive. During the month, railroad lines were linked up as much as possible to provide emergency outlets. For example, Tincourt and Quinconce through Buire and Doingt.[29]

France, 2-24-18
Acknowledgement mail One from Connie, Jan. 28, two from Papa, Jan. 18 Jan. 9 which contained money.

Dearest Mother: I am writing you a letter – not from France but from myself. That is the kind you like best, I know. Letters about France only widen the gulf. Letters from me bring us closer. I feel that difference when I write. It has a psychological effect on both of us I am sure.

Sometimes I may write mood things. Don't take exception to them. As a rule they are trivial and pass like of a gust of wind. I wrote you a letter on Washington's Birthday, which I hope does not reach you. I was in a sorry frame of mind about my financial condition, and intimated that I might wire for more money. I shall wire, but only in receipt of the postal order for forty dollars, which came yesterday. It is sufficient for my present needs. I have broken my allotment and I shall get results from it in two months. I shall be on my "financial feet" by that time. I have decided to wait two or three months until I take my leave, unless something unexpectedly turns up. In the meantime I shall indulge in two-penny "passes" to my old stomping ground. I may not mention the name of the place here, but you probably know where it is. I shall take my longer leave when sunny France is faithful to her name. *(He was probably in Amiens.)*

I have changed much since I have been out here. Of course I went through several revolutions, mental of course, before I adapted myself to the new conditions. Perhaps you have detected the conflict in my letters. I know I have many conflicting statements. I am still learning. New doors open at every turn of my

---

[29] Ibid., pp. 81–82

experience and I suffer another revolution of ideas. Perhaps you will not agree with the things I realize every day, but I think you will. My puritanical spirit resented the new order of things as I first saw them but I am understanding as I go. Things that were once repulsive are becoming mere facts which I may look upon with no disgust, analyze, and balance.

My views of religion, morality, and life have all changed – none to the worse, I hope, but I feel more at ease, more myself, I feel a burden lifted. Of course, I am unsteady, unsettled in many things, but on the whole, I feel broader, more sympathetic, more tolerant.

I have not been in a church but three times since I left the States *(here, he forgets Amiens though he had definitely been there by then, but perhaps not for a service)*. When I was on the coast of France, I attended a Catholic mass in a cathedral. The place was dim, altars, draperies, robes, all the extravagant symbols of the church were splendid, beautiful, soothing. The chanting of the choir, deep-toned and inspiring was restful, the people who came and knelt and prayed, the black-veiled women who stood half-concealed by the pillars of the domes and wept for someone who lay on the field of the Marne or Aisme, left the atmosphere wholly religious, and I myself felt the irresistible call of worship. I felt no stringent demand of doctrine – I forgot the creed, the incriminations, the Catholic church itself. I thought of God.

Again, I was near the front. The church was a deserted barn. I thought of the manger. The guns roared and fretted, and broke again into thunder. There're but a few of us, and we sang hymns, and a minister of Church of England spoke a few words. That was all of the service – it was the service of a direct opponent of the Catholic church, but I forgot the creed, and thought of God.

And now there is no church except all out-of-doors, and as I whistle down the track in the morning, I may think of God – that is, love and life, and pray in my spirit to be part of it all. That is religion too, shorn of all red tape, and the religion I aspire to.

I just now received the book of poems Miss Harriman sent me, and yesterday I received the Christmas Book ___ she mentioned in her last letter. She is too good to me. I know I do not reciprocate as I should. Some day perhaps, I can. Her friendship is an inspiration. If I can only crystallize the inspiration!

Sometimes I hope to write something worth while for your sake, and the sake of others who do so much for me. I have been writing but so futile are my efforts, they amount to so little. When I read the poems Miss Harriman sends me, I think there is little use. When I learn to live as those men have lived, perhaps I too may write something worthwhile. It is the living, after all.

How much I must learn! When I return to school, I shall make this experience amount to something more than a thorough soaking in the bitter in life and a good scrubbing with the rough side of it. Perhaps this little sojourn into the world will leave me rougher and world wiser, but I know I shall be bigger and broader –

I am going to write some more verse as I feel the inclination and shall try to send it as I write it.

With love to all of you, I am your son, Hubert

PS I shall have some pictures taken when I go on pass next week.

Tuesday, March 5, 1918

Dearest Mother: My leave came sooner than I anticipated, and now I am in Paris. I have been here three days, and what time I have not tramped about alone, I have been sleeping. I left the front Saturday at noon and arrived here Sunday morning in a snow storm. The weather is most unfavorable for sight seeing, but I have been making the most of it, walking the streets in exploration, or riding the "Metro." Otherwise known as the "tube" or "subway." It is a three-railed underground system of metropolitan streetcars. For fifteen centimes, one may be whisked to any part of the city. I have happened on many places of interest since I have been here – the "Latin Quarter," the Seine, Notre Dame, Place de Bastille. I was alone, I recognized the places and verified them by some Frenchman. I can make myself understood. That is how I get along by myself. I went through Notre Dame. It is being sand bagged as the cathedral of Amiens, and, of course, the façade is marred, but the interior was there – that was enough. I should attempt a description, I am too nervous. I shall wait until I return to the peaceful front.

I went out to 18 Avenue Parmentier to see papa's friend, Mr. Rossbach, and felt as if I were at home when I saw the sign "Sullivan Madiniere Compagnie." A little mademoiselle ushered me into the office, after I told her my name was "Kelley," she wrote it as "Calais." Mr. Rossbach was not in. I was told in excellent English, by the man in charge, that he was in South Africa. I decided not to wait for him.

The gentleman then asked me whether I had just come over. I was proud to say that I had been at the front nearing seven months. Very few Americans can say that. He was highly pleased. He took my "life history," and promised to write Mr. Rossbach immediately.

(Exit)

Paris is a wonderful city. We are given a warm reception everywhere we go — restaurants, theatres, shops — and all. I mean to take in some good shows while I am here. L'Opera Comique, L'Opéra, Alhambra, and the Casino. I couldn't go to any of the above last night. I went to the Olympia — a cheap vaudeville, a conglomeration of French and English. It was poor. I stood up in the promenoir for 2.60 fr.

Forgive the haste and incoherence. I can hardly think clearly. I shall write again soon.

Hubert.

France
March 8, 1918

Dearest Mother: I promised to write you again before I left Paris. I am sending this letter direct to New York by C.A. Rich, a sailor on the ship "Grant." He is a Kansas City boy, and of course during his brief stay in Paris we have been navigating the crooked streets together. Of course I am breaking regulation by sending this uncensored, but you can in a small way extenuate the crime by keeping the letter at home. I shall tell nothing that would endanger us though, I hope.

You may well know that this trip has been welcome, for I have been at the front nearing seven months, and I have seen almost as much as any American troops in France. Our regiment was one of the first in the Yankee troops to be under enemy fire. I left the States for Halifax, Nova Scotia, on July twenty-eight and on August twenty-eighth I was under fire. That is quite an experience, is it not?

Before I came on leave, I lived in a fever of anticipation and worry, even as I did when I was just a little kid. If I woke up in the night, and heard the put-put-put of the machine guns in the line, or the angry bark of the guns at Roisel, I would say, "Well, here goes my pass. The drive has started."

Fortunately I got out of Tincourt in a blizzard Saturday [March 3] at noon and rode to Amiens in a box car, a distance of some forty miles, but I did not get to my destination till seven o'clock in the evening, and was unable to get a bed. I walked the dark streets for an hour, stopping at hotels to be turned out with the slang refusal, "Napoo." I finally got into an "Estaminet" on condition I had a glass "vin blanc." I took the vin blanc and stayed till midnight, when I got standing-room to Paris; I go back up the line Sunday and although it is going to be hot soon, I really want to get back. I see evidence of a coming offensive every day. The Italians (those who refused to fight on the Piave) are digging trenches around our huts, and barbed wire is being strung in long lines around the slopes of the downs. I think we are to strike first, "Cambrai" is to be repeated, perhaps, but without the reaction.

I am very proud to have participated in the Cambrai offensive and defense. I was there! That was all though. I am only an insignificant time-keeper. We were not caught in the curve of the Boche, but we were at the edge of it. We were shelled, and also bombed on numerous occasions. I won't say "we," but bombing occurred in the near vicinity. Much is attributed to us that is undeserved.

You folks keep assuming that I am with the Americans. Not so! Our regiment is attached to the British, and we are the only Americans on that northern sector. Sometimes itinerant pioneer companies build bridges up our way, but seldom. My company is detached and is stationed with another company at the end of a narrow gauge, which operates up to the trench.

We are British. We speak a combination of English and American; that is, we swear in both languages; smoke British issue cigarettes and eat British rations. Some drink British rum! That's how they keep their nerve.

You will notice that this penmanship is rather rapid. Paris is very fast. I shall write you of it when I return to the peaceful front. It is serene up there. I have left the impression that all is blood and thunder up there – Not so! We are in the country there. There is a beautiful wood near our camp – the wood of Hennessy Chateau. I think that is the way to spell his name. I have heard it pronounced only. His chateau is a pile of debris, but the woods, though unkempt and wild, are beautiful.

Note the individual dedication at the bottom. That means I am out of francs and can't send souvenirs. (*This is written down the side of the letter on the last page.*)

Do not worry. I am several kilo behind the trenches. We are not undergoing unendurable hardships – a soldier never does. He is a lazy and immoral wretch in the long run, although some of them make great sacrifices and are noble.

Remember I am having a glimpse of life, a taste of experience, and shall soon return stronger in body, more willing to learn, and more able to appreciate a good square meal. Love to Connie, Grace, Kathleen, Ouida, and Dad. Your son, HWK. Give my love to Miss Harriman and Miss Boggess.

During March, the situation steadily became more tense. German prisoners and aerial observation all confirmed that a big drive was about to be launched. On March 14, Colonel Collins, the British commander, called a conference with the commanding officers of the light railway to discuss what should happen if communication lines were put out of action—as they indeed were almost as soon as the offensive begun.[30] Leave privileges were stopped in March and not resumed until November.[31]

France

3-12-18, Tuesday

Dearest Mother; I have been to Paris on leave as you already know and I am about to fulfill my promise of writing to you at normal speed of penmanship. I am not in a frantic haste as I was in Paris. I feel at perfect leisure and the hut is quiet. A few francs are being clinked at a poker game below me, but poker is a quiet conservative sort of game, and the noise is no bother.

You may notice omissions among the list of sights which I named as inferior to my meals, such inspiring places as Louvre, Luxembourg, Trocadero and Cluny museum. They were closed. Many of the notable arches and statues were sandbagged, and of course invisible, while the most precious pictures were sent away. That may seem discouraging, but do not think I missed what might be seen. I tramped Rivoli Boulevarde at its length, I roamed the Tuilleries, wandered through the Latin Quarter. I did not walk up on it intentionally. I found myself in it, and of course sought out "Notre Dame" on the "Citi." I am so sorry that I did not stay there longer. The fact is, I saw Notre Dame in one of her worst moods. I had heard she was gloomy, almost sinister, and I walked upon her on a wintry day, when the streets were mucky and the skies were gray, and every gargoyle had soft snow in his nostrils. She was indeed a wretched spectacle. The interior would have been too dark for human eyes, had not several candles burned like golden points in the gloom. After our eyes became accustomed to the darkness, the whole thing bloomed like the dawn, and in the dim twilight we beheld the high vaulted interior, the magnificent altar, the solemn rows of dark shiny mahogany pews, and the chaste marble of saints glimmering white in the dimness around the outer edges of the aisle, which encircled the interior and embraced the high altar and its worshipful tiers of seats, were the forbidding iron gratings of the shrines. And above all of it, vague in the wonderful complication of color, we beheld the multi-colored mosaic glass of the windows of Notre Dame. They were subdued, their dim light was religious, but I cannot

---

[30] Ibid., pp. 83–84.
[31] Ibid., p. 194.

-74-

describe them. I cannot visualize them; I only have the consciousness of having seen something beautiful and vague as the windows of heaven itself.

As I left the church with my comrade, the beggars stretched out their trembling hands. The souvenir vendors thronged about us with their cheap wares, and the sisters of the poor shook their boxes in our faces. They are wise to take advantage of the opportunities offered at the portals of Notre Dame for a man inevitably feels deep emotions throbbing through him as he leaves the place, but I hate to see God imposed on.

I went to Versailles with a mob of military tourists, and we were herded through the Chateau of Louis XIV. It was presented to us by a very business-like, matter of fact guide, and, of course, it was the most unromantic trip imaginable. We clattered up the grand staircase down which Louis and his court had often swept, and streamed through several rooms of which I do not remember the names. However, we eventually entered the Hall of Battles, a most war-like place. The walls are hung with pictures of the important and victorious battles of France, including Tours, Austerlitz, a conference of Washington, Lafayette, and Rochambeau and Wag…..The reception hall was visited at length and was really the most impressive room in the building. It is decorated as our elaborate reception and dance halls in the States, the frequent panels of glass, the stenciled walls, the pictured ceiling, the pendant chandeliers, and polished floor. If the chandeliers were not removed with the silver candle holders which projected from the walls, and at frequent intervals, the place would appear ready for the ball. It looks as if it had just been completed, it is so well-preserved. However, the glass panels are made of some of the first glass ever made, and brought over the Alps from Venice before railways were thought of. The whole building, in fact, was constructed from marble before the days of railways, and there is not an indigenous fragment of marble in France. At each end of the reception hall is an adjoining room, one of War, the other of Peace. They are both small rooms, each containing a council table. The room of war is dim, red, and gloomy. The ceiling is split with gilded fangs of lightening [sic], while swords and coats of mail figure the walls, and the followers of Mars, bearded and brutal, menace and threaten with pointed clubs. The last room we entered was the chapel of Louis, and we stood in the balcony where he and his Queen sat in state during services, and at the opposite end we beheld the high altar where the priest offici-ated, while the audience, contrary to custom, turned their backs to the cross, and faced Louis their Lord. As we thronged out the doors of the chapel and some of the boys stopped to buy souvenirs, I chanced to lean idly in a stone corner by the door, and noticed that the stone felt unusually rough on my head. Turn[i]ng about, I found the stone had been chipped away, where upon the guide, noticing my curiosity, told me I stood in the position of a Swiss Guard, and that the stone had been chipped away by the spears which were leaned there year after year.

Paris as a whole is too artificial. Its multitudes prey upon tourists, the relics are preserved for tourists, its thousands of hotels are made for tourists. I do not like the insincere spirit of obsequity [*sic*] which prevails. Of course the war has changed things much, but the old parasites still remain, and the Americans are the victims.

I wish I had the time [to] write more of what I saw but I must save it for another time. My bunkie has "retired" and I must follow toute suite. I shall make a list of letters received on a subsequent page.

I am enclosing a picture of "L'Ange Pleureur," a statue which I saw in a cathedral of which I have written before. I saw this on my return from Paris, and was very much impressed by it. I sent Connie a large photograph of it – The Weeping Angel.

Up to date, I have received: Connie, Feb. 17, Connie's – Feb. 18, Papa's – Feb. 19, Mama's Feb. 20, Mama's and Grace's of Feb. 12, Kathleen's of Jan. 11. With love, Hubert

On March 21, 1918, at 4:30 a.m., the enemy attack began; communications were knocked out at Tincourt, Quinconce, and Fins so they worked in isolation. The 24th Division British fought hard but the Germans had numerical superiority. They searched out mid and rear areas for dumps, camps, roads, railroads, and gun positions.[32]

The Twelfth had to evacuate the camps at Quinconce and Fins. On March 21, Tincourt crews had salvaged 35 cars and taken them with them in the retreat.[33]

On March 22, they rerailed some cars. Men from Companies D and F were sent back to Quinconce to load coal, dismantle and bring back the huts, and clean out the ammunition dump. The Tincourt camp was evacuated that day when they heard from a dispatch rider that the British infantry was in full retreat through Roisel.[34] *Finally, on March 24, the majority of men from all companies were assembled as a unit at La Flaque, where the enemy had conducted many bombing raids. At 3 Aa.m. on March 25, the regiment moved to*

---

[32] Ibid., p. 87.
[33] Ibid., p. 94.
[34] Ibid., p. 95.

The Weeping Angel, in Amiens
Cathedral

Vecquemont, a distance of 22 kilometers. In preparation for retreat, the men stripped the trains of injectors and side bars and the tractors of carburetors.[35]

On March 26, everyone left Vecquemont and marched through Daors, Pont Noyelles, Behencourt, Contray, and Vadencourt, a distance of 18 kilometers, in less than 8 hours. There they received orders to march to Valheureux, 18 kilometers farther on. They arrived at midnight, after covering 22 miles that day and 14 miles the day previous. The resumed the march the next day, arriving in Terramesnil at 5 p.m., where they were assigned billets—in this case, stable space.

The regiment was able to replace some of the equipment and clothing which had been lost in the Somme during the retreat.[36]

At Terrasmenil, they built trenches for the Pas-Conde defense system.[37]

See Letter to Ouida, November 29, 1918, for HWK's description of the battle as he experienced it.

---

[35] Ibid., p. 98ff.
[36] Ibid., pp. 104–105.
[37] Ibid., p. 106.

Monday, April 1, 1918
Somewhere in France

Dear Mother: I am writing under the queerest of circumstances. Forgive the form. The candle is dim, and a barn full of hay does not afford the best facilities for correspondence.

Your package (observe the stationery) came this evening, and I was delighted to find that it contained a towel – a lovely towel – Pourquoi? Because I have no towel nor anything else. I may not answer all of your letters (I think I have received them all) for they are lost too, all my books are gone, but happily I received "On the Day of Battle" from Miss Harriman several days ago. I can pack it about with one in my haversack.

I sent the clipping from the *K.C. Post and Star*. There were too many jumps between thoughts, and oh, so much left out. I wrote you a letter one memorable evening (I doubt whether it ever reached you) and told you that two of my poems "Cambric" and "Roisel Road" were printed in the "New York Herald." I sent you a paper containing "Roisel Road" at the same time. I have never been able to obtain one containing "Cambric" although it was printed. I am to receive two hundred francs for the two verses. As soon as I get settled down again I shall write more. I have some real tales to tell now, for I have seen and lived real life –

With love, Hubert

April 4, 1918

Dearest Mother: You must be tired of my eternal apology, but again I must say that the barn is too dim for writing, and it is drizzling outside. The page may be smeary.

I can write nothing interesting in this envelope, much less in a censored one, so bear with me. I shall discuss purely personal matters. They are all we can discuss in these stirring days.

The other day when we were working, the captain called me out of the trench I was digging and gave me a clipping from the Kansas City Journal in which the verse "Cambric" was printed. I was very glad to read the comment the Journal made. I wonder if you saw it – "a singularly well-composed and dignified little lyric which may be classed among the best of recent war poems." I am not boasting; merely telling you something which you may have missed. I know it will be as much satisfaction to you as to me.

I have been unable to get any more copies of the New York Herald, although two of my verses were printed. That is hard luck, is it not?

Hereafter my correspondence may be stinted. I don't think I shall have the opportunity to write anything lengthy. I can only tell you things of a very indirect character.

Please tell Miss Harriman that I have received, "The Hound of Heaven," Lionel Johnson's "Poems," "Francis Ledwidge," "Christmas Edition of the Bookman," and "Diary and Letters of Alan Seeger" from her, and that although they were all lost, I certainly appreciated and enjoyed them all. I have "In the Day of Battle" in my possession.

Tell Miss Boggess that I shall answer her last letter as soon as possible. Give her my warmest regards.

If you did not get my last letter, I received the box containing candy, cocoa, sugar, towel, stationery, "goods of questionable character," etc.

With love, Hubert

France

April 10, 1918

Dearest Mother: I received your letter of March 9 two days ago, and Papa's letter of March 8 (in answer to my cable) came at the same time. I have heard nothing since.

I appreciated the clippings you sent, although I had already seen one of them. I am sorry that the verse "Cambric" was published. "The New York Herald" has asked for the copyright, and of course, the previous publication of it will probably make it impossible to sell.

I hate to talk about the verses forever. I should be writing new ones, but we have only a lantern to write by – one lantern and a barnful of straw does not offer very favorable accommodations for serious scribbling. However, a letter from a nurse in Italy was published in the "N.Y.H" on "Roisel Road." She said, along with a few minor things, that she thought it the best verse published in the contest. I thought you would appreciate that. The copyright goes to the "N.Y.H." for a hundred francs.

As soon as I get the opportunity I shall work hard on some new verses. I have so many new things to write about.

I wish I could tell you a few things I have seen and experienced. They _____ through everything else I have told you in the sphere of commonplace.

Perhaps someday I shall have a new trophy for your collection, if not this time, some other time when the opportunity presents itself. One of our Lieutenants said he was going to recommend several of us for military medals. I wish I could tell you the occasion, but I am forbidden. Keep this to yourself.

I wish you would not publish any of my letters – those I have written nor those I mean to write. As to the verses I sent you (most of which are inconsequential) do not publish them. You will understand. I once said I did not care, but I do. I am not sorry that you have published what you have. All of that is inconsequence. Enough of this.

I got a letter from Harry Sheskin yesterday. I shall write to him tomorrow. I invite him over occasionally to eat. He can fill my chair once in a while. He a great boy [*sic*].

Kiss the kids for me. Connie must think I have forgotten or neglected her, but far from it. She is the subject of some of my best thoughts. With love, Hubert

P.S. I got some milk at a farm house today, and used some of the cocoa you sent me. It was worth all the trouble I took to make it.

The fortifications were finished on April 10. On April 11, the regiment moved to Val de Maison, where they seem to have stayed until April 16, when they went to Woirel, a two-day march through Talmas, Naours, Haverny, Canaples, Halley, Bertheaucourt, and St. Ouen. They spent a night at the edge of Flexcourt after 16 miles in the mud and rain. The next day in the cold and wet, they marched 14 miles through Bourdon, Hangest, Soues, le Quesnoy, and Airaines, arriving in Woirel in the evening.[38]

April 19, 1918, France

Dear Mother: Can't write much. I am well and living a real soldier's life. The enclosed is self-explanatory. Get a copy when it comes out, and let me have it.

I shall send something new soon. Hubert

April 19–21 were spent resting, cleaning equipment, and getting ready to build railroads. On April 22, the Second Battalion, which

---

[38] Ibid., p. 111.

included Company D, started work on the preparation of the road bed for a second track on the Longpre–Gamaches Railway Line. There was the probability of the regiment being used as infantry to strengthen the British line should the enemy renew its drive on the Channel ports. Therefore more time and effort was devoted to infantry drill, bayonet exercise, and target practice.[39]

May 2, 1918 France

Dearest mother: I have tried to answer the last mail I received for three evenings, but every time I tried I found myself too tired. I have a new tablet tonight, and that may be impetus enough to carry me through a whole letter.

In the first place, I received letters as follows: Mamma – April 1 and April 5, Connie March 30 and April 1, Kathleen April 1, Papa April 1, I hate a receipt – Some how I can't do justice to it. Tell Harry I received another letter from him dated March 27 – You may be surprised to know that Grover wrote me too.

I shall not write for anything; the method of procedure is too complicated. I am in good financial circumstances since I received the order from you and the check from the Herald, and I can buy some few things from the civilians.

You should not have written to the Herald. I am dealing with the European Edition. Of course the verses may appear in the American Edition. I am enclosing a letter which may interest you.

I have been writing very little, but I am thinking much. I wrote one verse the other day but it was not worth the copying. I mean to write several as soon as they shape themselves.

We are at the edge of a beautiful wood with a town at the foot of the road; and a white chateau with a wide lawn glimmers like an old colonial mansion through the trees on the slope beyond the village. We never hear a gun. They are too far away.

Give my regards to [M]iss Harriman and Miss Boggess, and tell Harry I shall write.

With love, Hubert

---

[39] Ibid., p. 113.

France

May 12, 1918

Dear Mother: I have pondered all afternoon over this letter, and gaining nothing, I have resolved to write as ever in a spontaneous scribble. A man's thoughts take order and shape, yet before he sets them down, he finds a thread of the "forbidden" tangled in the fabric of his theme and he writes not.

This is Mother's Day and that is why I am so anxious to write you something cheering and of good form, but I know you love every mis[s]hapen line that comes from France.

I had thought to write you a verse but verses are not every day occurrences, so do not blame me, blame the muse. Had this been a more pleasant day, I might have invoked her, but, alas, the winds bloweth chilly blasts over the fields, so have I spent my day in the tent smoking the vile weed in divers [*sic*] forms and reading what seemed most pleasant to my eye and fancy.

Despite the discomfort of the weather, the French are strolling the way and pass the camp in curious throngs. Some are fair to behold, and sometimes I am tempted to step out of the "Sibley," and promenade with some fair damsel, but my trousers are rent, and my face not good to behold for the French sun hath wrought havoc with my complexion. So must I refrain, and sit in my tent and think morose thoughts which do border on wrath.

I had a letter from Norman Meier, who is not in my caste, and therefore it is with deep consideration that I answer him. He is in France acting as Master Engineer in some obscure unit.

Our mail is slow of late, as I write without acknowledging any mail I have not received. (These lines are becoming complicated so I shall lapse me into serious English again, if such a thing is possible under these conditions.)

Tell Miss Harriman and Miss Boggess that I have not forgotten them, and that I shall write eventually. All I can say to you folks at home is here, so I will write to the rest. It would be idle repetition.

Tell Clarence to let me know when he lands – that is, immediately. He might come to me or I go to him under the present circumstances. Sometimes I wish I were with him, but I suppose things must be as they are. (There is a thread of fatalism. Pretty far gone, eh?)

How goes Connie's aviator? Leading a high life perhaps. He'll come to earth apres la guerre. With Love, Hubert

5-19-18, France

Dearest Mother:

I was in a town near here today and while there I sent you a card and Kathleen a few little French books which may help her in her studies. When I returned, weary and disgusted, I was mail shocked to find several letters awaiting me.

Kathleen (April 16), Connie (April 21–28), You (April 15, 26)

I am tired but I know I shall be less able to write tomorrow night so I must take advantage of the opportunity. You mentioned Kathleen's story. I received a copy of it, and answered once concerning it, but I suppose you did not get it. The story was excellent for a kid – but I mean to tell her.

I am so sorry you moved. You are farther away than ever now. I had begun to live at the other place, but here I must accustom myself to a new environment. That balcony, overlooking the back yard sounds pleasant to my ears, and that may redeem the situation.

Ben Johnson has landed in France! If he knows my address and does not write, me thinks he is inconsiderate but I suppose he does not know my regiment. Send me his address, will you?

I had several pictures taken today. They will be ready in a week, and if they are respectable, they shall be sent. The French are miserable photographers. Three I had taken with Newby, and six I had single. If he finishes them as they should be finished, there will be very little of the visage left for, as I said before, the French suns are fertile with freckles. I met a little freckled face French kid and could have kissed him for his trouble. With love, HWK

May 23, 1918

Dear Mother: Just a scratch to relieve your anxiety. I am still knocking about, and fancy I shall continue to do so for some time to come. The "Tommy" is either knocking about, or the cleats [?] in his shirt are knocking about, or he is inquiring whether there is a wee bit of fuel knocking about to build a blooming fire with.

The other day one of our sergeants made a "flying switch" despite the protest of an English officer, "— It can't be done." It was done, whereupon the officer said, "Clevah! What part of the States did you come from?" "Kansas City," came the abrupt reply.

"Kansas?" ejaculated the officer.

"H____, no! Missouri!" was the disgusted response.

"Ah, have a cigarette," said the frustrated Britisher.

I hope you appreciate that as I did when I heard it. It struck my funny bone.

I had my picture taken Sunday, and I shall send it next week. I hope it is good – but I told you that once. I received Grace's letter of the twenty-sixth and shall answer it. That may make her angry, but I shall answer it sometime, and regain her favor.

I sent K. some books to the old address but I suppose they will be sent to the house.

With beaucoup love, Hubert

France

June 2, 1918

Dear Mother: Here are the pictures! If I had not promised them, I would not send them, for, unfortunately the photographer failed to eradicate all the facial camouflage. I do look a bit like a Boche, and, as a complimentary comrade said, like the typical amazon of the Russian Battalion of Death. Let it be as it is!

I am well and in soldierly spirits. Your letters of the fourth and seventh of May came safely sealed. Give Ouida and Junior my best love, and tell the teachers I shall write eventually. With love, Hubert

France

June 10, 1918

Dear Mother: I just had two letters from you, one from Connie, and one from Grace all dated the second week of May. The packages you mentioned have not arrived, but I suppose they will be here eventually if Jones said he would get them over.

I just came off guard an hour ago, and am rather tired, to say the least. The guard was worthwhile though. I found a Century for December in one of the guard tents, and learned who my friend, Herbert Adams Gibbons, is.[40] He is a war authority residing in Paris, and among his most notable works is "Paris Reborn: The New Map of Europe." It is remarkable too. (I found an article on

---

[40] Herbert Adams Gibbons edited a book of WWI poetry, *Songs from the Trenches*, in 1918 (Harper & Brothers). Three of HWK's poems were published in it.

Hubert and Fred M. Newby

the beginning of the chapter on the American troops that gave his works and his present capabilities. That's why I know.)

In the same magazine I discovered the article, "Solemn-looking Blokes," which concerned our march through London. Send for it in booklet form. The Century put it out at first in a pamphlet. It would make a good "Dec" [*sic*] or at least an inspiration for Grace's "Oration" next year. I am so sorry she didn't win a medal but those are idle words. She won something greater than a medal and she knows it.

Tell Kathleen to tackle the verse again next year, and that if she wants to discuss I.S.C. with me, write earlier. This thing was over this year before she had informed me. She meant to try verse. Of course the mail was late. Of course!!

This is such a miserable letter, and I won't apologize for my laziness. I haven't been writing to anyone but you folks there at home, and I've been negligent in that this last week or so. I'll try to do better.

I weighed [myself] several days ago and I weigh one hundred forty in the clothes I wore in the pictures I sent you. I never felt better in my life.

I sent K. some little books on primary French, but I think I addressed them to the other house. I suppose she has advanced far beyond them now.

With all the love in the world, Hubert.

In early June, the Twelfth began to lay steel on the section between Wiry and Oisemont. All of the grading was done by hand. The material was all clay and chalk, and the waste was handled by light railway dump cars to the fills, the cars being moved by hand. The hauls were as great as 800 to 1,000 feet. Work was seriously affected in June when an epidemic of Spanish flu broke out, but there were no deaths or serious side effects to the men. [41]

June 13, 1918

Dearest Mother: I shall attempt to write that long-neglected letter which I have been promising for several weeks. I did not work as strenuously as I might have today, and I feel disposed. Again the letters which came to-day are some incentive. Papa's letter of May sixteenth with your letter of the fifteenth came this evening.

I cannot say that the clipping you sent me was as interesting as it might have been. I could send you one as interesting though. The town mentioned was very familiar to me.

You asked me about the boy, Raymond. I met him in Paris, and have heard nothing of him since I left there. I came upon him in a curious crowd which had gathered at the scene of the previous night's bombing disaster. He spoke some English and accosted me as if he had known me all my life. After completely satisfying our morbidity, we strolled over to the Brentano's Book Shop where I relieved myself of the only responsibility I had in the city – that of buying our former captain a "Guide of Southern France." Raymond made me believe that he was at my service, and insisted on guiding me to my destination. I had none, so we took out on a vagrant stroll. We walked till noon, when he telephoned his instructor that he had decided to "play hooky." He attended school somewhere in the environs of Paris where he was specializing in foundry work. His school corresponded to our high school, with the exception of the period of "servitude" – three years. He was to finish this May, as nearly as I could understand, at the age of seventeen. (We had some difficultly in making ourselves clear on some points.)

I was with him only that day, and when he went to my room, I ask[ed] him to write to the "Duchess" [*His sister, Kathleen.*] I did not intend to be the means

[41] Laird, *History of the Twelfth*, p. 115ff.

Receipt dated 5/6/1918

of bringing two kindred spirits together, or of starting an overseas romance; I merely meant to give K.W.K. some incentive in studying "Francais." (I don't believe the French capitalize that. Ask the Soph. She knows.)

I have promised him some books and magazines to help him in English, but the great push broke my promise. I lost everything I intended to send; I even lost his address. I believe I have a right to detail the Duchess: to either make my word good, or send me the address, that I may do so.

I should like to have Ben Johnson's address. He should know mine, but it seems that he doesn't for I haven't heard a word from him. I think a glimpse of someone I have known would make me a better man. (Note that underscore. I can swing a pick with the best of them.)

I suppose Grace is well on her way to the golden sunset now. That is where I might have been, but had I gone, she could not have made the trip. I shall go someday – and farther with you.

Uncle Phil wrote me on the sixteenth, and made me feel as if he still knew me. Perhaps he can't say as much for me. He expects to return to K.C. "tout-d'suite." (We say – "tootsweet." I have never seen it written out. Maybe "Cinderella" can enlighten you or me.)

I was talking to one of our men out on the works today, and he showed me a picture of his girl standing somewhere on Kavanaugh mountain near Poteau. (*Hubert Kelley was born in Poteau, OK.*) He lives there, while she was born there twenty years ago. Her name is Christine Williams. Do you know her?

With love, Hubert

June 27, 1918

Dearest Mother: I am afraid Ouida and Grace are on their way or I would answer their letters – June 4 and May 20 respectively. The box from "Au bon Marche," Paris came day before yesterday. It was a pleasant surprise. I saw the store when I was in the city. I do not think you get your money's worth by ordering through Jones. I wish you wouldn't do it. I am drawing my pay now, and behind lines can get what I need.

I am in the best of health, and am confident you are the same. Clarence is a lucky dog but I suppose he will soon be over. I may get to be with him when he comes. If I can possibly transfer to his unit, I shall do so – if he doesn't mind. I want to hear the guns again. An older brother could claim his younger one if he goes about it right.

Edgar Thorpe's case certainly made me sick. I never felt any sorrier for a kid in my life. He is foolish, but what an impossible _____ to the girl and the mother-in-law.

I'm glad you got the contest straight at last. I didn't know you had received the "Heralds."

Give my love to Harry, Miss Harriman, Miss Boggess, and the whole family.

Your Son, Hubert

France

July 1918

Dearest Mother: Just a few words! A rain storm is coming and it is almost dark. I have had seven letters since June 11, the last one being June 24.

I am in the best of health although I weigh only 130 lbs. stripped. I shall pick up in the winter. Grace is getting fat, according to her letters.

Tell Harry I received his last two letters – one of June 20, and that I will write soon.

With love, Hubert. P.S. Forgive the length – I am lazy.

On July 4, the British awarded military decorations to several members of the 12th Engineers in recognition of their distinguished conduct during the Somme defensive. In his speech at the ceremony, Major General RU.H. Buckland of the British Fourth Army noted that the American colonies had fought against the British for six years beginning in 1776. Since that time, history had demonstrated that America was right and England was wrong. The present war, he said, had lasted nearly four years, and it was significant that now England and America were fighting side by side in defense of the same principle for which Americans had fought in 1776.

He continued, "The Commanding General...would have been here himself today but he has been very busy. We had a little fight this morning which will likely interest you as some of your comrades [the 33rd Division] were instrumental in its success. The attack was made at 2 A.M. by the Australian Corps and the Americans. At the time I left Headquarters this morning, all objectives had been taken and 450 prisoners had been counted; but these figures will be increased as reports come in. The tanks played a very important part in the engagement and came back covered with wounded men singing and cheering like mad." [42]

France

July 6, 1918

Dearest Mother: Just a line to let you know that I am well, and that I am working more or less as the spirit moves me. I received all the mail between May 20 and June 11, the receipt of which was missing in the last letter, because the delinquent postman skipped three weeks. If you wish a capitulation of dates, I will try to get to the bottom of my haversack for the letters in question.

I am so glad that we now have a builder of ships in the family. Keep up the good work, trust in God, and carry on! (*Hubert's father went to work in the New Orleans Shipyard.*)

The package Kathleen sent from Paris has not arrived. It will drift along

---

[42] Ibid., p. 121.

tout disunite [*sic*] I suppose as every thing else does. I am not hungry, though I was just down behind the white chateau and imbibed much to the discomfort of my inner tube, two gigantic bowls of milk from the pastures of Picardy.

The old Frenchman who lives at the "dairy" tips me the wink every time I enter his door. One day he was riding to his plow on his unshapely steed, and, wishing the horse to divert from the beaten path, cried, "Eep!" (I do not know the French orthography, but this is an anglicized picture of the word.) In the spirit of an echo, I answered, "Eep!" whereupon my Frenchman turned his mount, and galloped madly across the field, across the road, and drew halter at the very knife of my tent. I was deeply mortified, frightened, and several other things. I thought the old gentleman wanted to slay me or put in a claim for five thousand francs, but he merely dismounted, looked upon me with a red, beaming countenance, and whispered the one magic word, "Tabac!" I was all action. I dived in the tent, dived in my blue-bag, and produced more "Bull Durham" than the dear old fellow had seen since the Napoleonic wars. That is why the wink is tipped, the blue eyes twinkle, and the red countenance beams when I cross the threshold of the cottage behind the chateau.

With love to all the kids, I am, Your Son, HWK

> *On July 22, 1918. the 12th Engineers and Company D were ordered to depart from the British division they had served for almost a year and move from the Somme, departing by train from Longpre to Baccarat farther south. There they joined the American Expeditionary Forces.*[43]
>
> *At Badmenil, about a mile from Baccarat, the Twelfth set up camp. This was different from the Somme—there was plenty of water, farmers worked in their fields, and the artillery was usually quiet.*[44] *In Baccarat, however, once the 12th arrived, bombing began nightly—there had been an unwritten understanding that if the French did not attack certain towns in German territory, the Germans would not bomb Baccarat. The American airmen did not recognize this and bombed over the German line so Baccarat became a prime target.*
>
> *Company D was put into a camp in the woods, just west of Indian Village.*[45]

---

[43] Ibid., p. 124.
[44] Ibid., p. 134.
[45] Ibid., p. 133.

July 31, 1918

Dearest Mother – I have received about seven letters since I wrote last. Papa wrote from Pascagoula on July 1, and you may tell him how glad I was to get the letter. I would have written sooner, but I had to adapt myself to our new surroundings. We are with the Yanks now. The roar of guns is not as far distant now. We carry our masks these days.

You asked about the packages. I received both – one from you and one from Kathleen. As to the gold Chevrons you mentioned, we wear two now – something of which only fifteen thousand may boast. [*Soldiers received one stripe, a "gold chevron," for each six months served in Europe.*]

Will you do me a favor? Perhaps Connie could do it easily. I promised the girl in England a book on the technique of the short story. I promised her one from Paris, but Brentano's had none. Connie has studied short story, so she should be able to judge what books would be best. She might write her a letter.

Miss Flossie Aston, 74 Albert Road, Handsworth, Birmingham, England. Thanks!!

Tell C. there is L'Ecole of the district two doors down from my billet. The children are very young; some mere tots. The studying goes on aloud. Would it not be an experience to teach with the guns punctuating your sentences with their hoarse grunts. It is said that farther north on the Verdun and Rheims sectors, the children attend their underground academies equipped with gas masks and tin-hats. That would be something worth while to impress on her wayward or delinquent imps.

I've been reading some O Henry the last few days. Pretty good on the whole! I've read "The Gentle Grafter," "Options," and the "Voice of the City" so far, and if the K. of C. supplies any other editions, I shall read them.

By the time this letter reaches home, I suppose Grace will have come back from Utah. When I heard that she was contemplating the trip, she was there, and when I hear she has gone, she is back.

This morning the town crier made his rounds in a gold-braided uniform of Blue, and called out the inhabitants with a trap-drum. They swarmed from every conceivable shelter to hear his proclamation. Wooden shoes clattered down every highway and by-way and the peasants gathered in our court. I though he was doing it to order an evacuation. But after all his loud shouting and energetic *(Letter ends.)*

France

August 9, 1918

Dearest Mother: We are settled at last, deep in gloomy pines among the hills. I am very well pleased with our new location, and hope to thrive in fat and fancy on this mountain air.

I believe much of our fear that I do not get all your letters is due to my negligence in receipting all of my mail. I may be "somewhere else" when the mail comes, and somewhere else when I answer it, and sometimes only wet scraps remain of the once crisp correspondence. I do not say that is the rule; it sometimes happens, and that particular letter (or letters) becomes null, void, and unanswered. Sometimes I do not list the dates of mail received. That is gross neglect, but true.

I have on hand Connie's letter of July 6 (including a photo I am proud to exhibit), and from Grace, you, I have letters dating July 8, 11, and 12, while Ouida wrote me on July 4, and sent me a picture of a Salt Lake crowd preserving themselves in the brine. All three of our representatives looked as if war were yet unknown. It's hard to realize there are spots on earth where peace abides.

It is futile to discuss Ben's death. (*Ben Johnson died in France on June 7, 1918.*) You know it hurts me, for we were pals so long, but no one was more worthy of dying here in France than Ben, for I know he did it bravely, as he did everything. I have been looking forward to seeing him here in France, but if he be dead, I must look for his grave.

Tell Harry I received the book of Seeger's today, and that by the time this letter arrives, he should have received a letter from me.

I can say little more this time. I have written some verses which I shall send next time.

I received Clarence's snapshot from Ouida. He had what we call "beaucoup swank," but I remarked that after they dragged him over the muddy Somme for twelve months, he would take his blooming fag from between his tea-stained lips, and say with the rest of the troops, "I'm muddy, don't give a d___, and I'm fed up with the whole rotten carry-on." P.S. I've quit smoking. With love, Hubert

August 18, 1918

Dearest Mother: I am in the forest primeval, in all the solitude that Nature offers, and still I am only a hundred yards from our howling camp. I come here every day to read and scribble, and can almost believe, sometimes, that I am in a summer resort, and that Fritzie, sailing high above the trees through a cluster of white puffs of shrapnel smoke, like a bee among blossoms, is a spectacle arranged especially for my pleasure. When night comes, however, —— becomes an apparent illusion, for we arm ourselves and go on the long road to work. We are rather enjoying the life as we are living it now. We have plenty of leisure time. We are at a very invigorating altitude, and the mountain air is filtered through banks of pines before it reaches us.

I have been getting any number of 'Stars' of late, until I have a veritable firmament under the bed. Whether I shall ever read them all I do not know, but I have found quite a variety of uses for them, and they will not go to waste.

I found one of my books the other day, one which I had never read and which I believed to have been lost. When Jerry broke through I packed rather hastily, and was forced to leave part of my library for the flames, but whether I had packed it or not it would have been the same, for the baggage met a disastrous fate ere ceased the flight [sic]. However, I found "Rupert Brooke" on somebody's table the other day, and claimed it as mine own because of certain marks of identification thereon.

Grace and Kathleen should be in school by the time this reaches you. I suppose Kathleen will continue her French. If I ever take a notion, I believe I can learn it thoroughly in a short while, but how is a man to study here?

Clarence will probably come in this sector when he comes over, as this is "the beginning." Unfortunately we had "the end" first.

With love, Hubert

P.S. Put my number on all mail – 162, 260.

August 21, 1918

Dearest Mother: I am answering your letter, no, although it has not been fifteen minutes in my possession. Should I neglect it a day, the missive might be scattered on the four winds. I am speaking of your letter of the eighteenth of July.

It was with a mixture of emotions that I heard of Clarence leaving. I am glad to have one of the family over here, that we may possibly see each other, but on the other hand, I am afraid his expectations may be disappointed. But this war is serious, and a shattered hope or sacrifice of a life means nothing. So much for prosaic philosophy.

I am looking forward to going home to Pascagoula. I see no reason why you shouldn't move if the climate will better Grace's health, and the move be economic. As for any attraction Kansas City may have, I would prefer the coast any day. If you want my opinion of the matter, I say, "Let's go South." A southern sea shore always did appeal to me.

I got a letter from Grace today, dated the eighteenth and one from Connie dated the seventeenth. Since you are constantly in touch with Harry, I want to tell him that not only have his letters been received but that "Seeger" and the set of the "Roycroft" and "Contemporary Verse" have come also. I shall write when I have something worthwhile to say.

Forgive this mad scribble. I am a hurry for some inexplicable reason. I think it is to get through and have Pascagoula off my mind.

I am still getting the K.C. Star, and Miss Boggess is sending me the "New Republic."

Tell G. and K. that even though I have seemingly neglected them, I have really acknowledged most of their letters, and if they did not receive the receipts, it was the fault of someone else. I have been satisfying myself with one letter to the family as a whole, although I am sure my negligence is not very satisfactory to you. With love, Hubert

On August 25, the Second Battalion, with Company D, moved from Baccarat to the Toul sector. Company D went to Sorcy Gare.[46] Much of the work in Baccarat was abruptly discontinued, perhaps because the sector was jointly administered by the French and the Americans, who could not mutually agree on strategy.

France
September 4, 1918
Dearest Mother: I learned from your letter of July twenty-third, the last one I received, that Clarence was about to sail, but even at this late date I have seen nothing of him. I suppose he will drift into some foggy harbor some of these days, highly elated at arriving in the promised land at last.

You should be back from Hot Springs by this time, and well on your way to Pascagoula. If you did not get my last letter, you must understand that I am look-

---

[46] Ibid., p. 141.

ing forward to a quiet little haven on the sea shore when I return, and that even though my happiest remembrances are of Kansas City, I could stand the change right well. Where are you are, home is – so have no scruples about leaving.

Have you received the "Solemn-looking Blokes" from the Century yet? You said you had sent for it. You must know before you read it that the solemnity was not the result of "promethean fires," but the gnawing remembrance that we had had nothing to eat since two o'clock that morning, when we entrained for London. A soldier is much more solemn over the loss of one meal than even the evacuation of the Somme.

In Grace's last letter, which I acknowledged several weeks ago, she mentioned having some of my verses with her, and asked me to send what I had written since I had sent the last.

I am enclosing some rather spontaneous and juvenile scribbles which I wrote when we were in the pines. I am sending them at her special request, and not because I think that they are worth while.

Tell the mighty ship-builder that I am bunking with his friend D.D., and that our snoring is harmonious.

Most of these verses are on the paper on which they were originally written, and you may have to use an interpreter. Paper is scarce, however, and I was not able to copy them. They are not serious efforts, but good practice.

With love, Hubert

From the moment it began on September 12, the St. Mihiel offensive was a success. Men were able to work on extending the light railway system out of Rattentout to the German light railway system out of Mouilly, a town that was in ruins.[47] *During the preparations for the offensive, the Second Battalion (and Company D) was working with the 21st Engineers. They were comparatively new at the light railway "game," and authorities continually differed on methods and means. In retrospect, the men of the 12th called this period "Forty Days in the Wilderness."*[48]

---

[47] Ibid., p. 146.
[48] Ibid., p. 151.

France

September 19, 1918

Dear Kathleen: I used to call you "Little Sis," but I suppose your inches compare favorably with mine now. That was fourteen long months ago – ages, it seems to me. It seems strange that a year can mist the past as it does here. Everything I left is so remote from experiences I have had since the German drive in the Spring that I can hardly believe that it ever existed.

When a man has seen the country raked with shells, huts go up in flames, men fall around him, and has stood in No-Man's land with everything behind him and nothing but the mass formation of the Huns coming over the hills in front of him with only a pile of coal and a shovel to divert his mind, he is inclined to forget the easy going life he left. But that was months ago, and is better unsaid. We are living a very normal life at present. Outside of that, there is nothing to report.

I received Connie's tri-letter and the letter Mama sent on her return from Hot Springs. With love, Hubert

P.S. Everything you say is coherent.

P.P.S. Ask Connie who sent the service flag. She didn't say.

P.P.P.S. etc You never did send me a translation of Raymond's letter, or tell me whether you answered it or not.

September 20, 1918

Dearest Mother: Unfortunately I wrote yesterday, and here come two letters today, so in order to satisfy my conscience, I must answer now. Your letters were written on the sixteenth and twenty-first of August, some time ago, but they were from home, and that means everything.

I supposed you will be overjoyed to know that I just heard from Clarence. I am enclosing his letter. I just wrote him a half inch of pencil, and we are trying to get together.

I read your clipping concerning "the dead city of Picardy," and it was like the knowledge of a resurrection to me. I knew the city when it was alive. I have visited it some five or six times, and was there only two weeks before its temporary "death." It was like a fairy-land to me. Somehow I always walked on air through its streets. It was far too beautiful to be a reality.

The siren of Pascagoula is luring me already. The legend of the river increases my anxiety about your decision. I am afraid you will change your mind. But if malaria drives the family to New Orleans, you will be tangled up in such a predicament as mine. It is but a petit France, so they say.

I am glad Papa is on his feet again. I was worried about him. He can't afford to hold up the navigation. We must have our ships. When we get knocked out we get two compound cathartics and duty, if a leg is not missing.

With love, Hubert

Sept. 27, 1918

Dearest Mother: I have a strong table under my wrist, a clear candle and mind, a comfortable seat and a water tight dugout, but very little to write that could pass the censor with a quiet conscience. Not that I have been leading a life of thrills, but I have been leading such a commonplace sort of an existence out here that I could not make an interesting account of it without going into censorable details.

I had a long letter from Kathleen to-day, dated the twenty-second. I was glad to get Raymond Gariel's address. I lost it in the retreat, and wanted to write to him. I shall write immediately.

I have not heard from Clarence again. I wrote him a long letter some time ago, and should hear from it shortly.

With love, Hubert

On October 6, orders were issued to put the 12th Engineers in charge of the light railways in the Toul sector. The Twelfth took over from the 21st Engineers, and on October 7, Company D relocated to Sorcy Gare.[49] The Toul sector was so large that the 4th Battalion of the 21st Engineers was added, and the Twelfth was placed strictly on operating duty. There were 2,250 men in the Operating Division and 3,800 men in construction and maintenance for a total of 6,050 men in the sector.[50] As a result of the changes and the recaptured area, the 12th Engineers operated 1,034 square kilometers of track. While the track was in fair condition, track clearance had to be widened to accommodate American equipment.[51] Work was intense and continued through rain and snow.

---

[49] Ibid., p. 151ff.
[50] Ibid., p. 154–155.
[51] Ibid., p. 161.

Oct. 10, 1918

Dearest Mother: I am out of the pines, and in a busy little valley at the foot of some chalk hills. The place has too much of an industrial atmosphere. I despise anything of the kind.

Clarence has written one letter, which I told you of in a previous letter. I shall hear news of him soon, I suppose. I'll find him suddenly, as all things happen in France.

You did not tell me why Papa was in St. Louis. You told me he wrote that Col. Willing was there, and had published some interesting information.

I was delighted to hear that the book was published. I wished you had sent a description of it, but c'est bon as it is.

The remainder of the allotment was not to be sent, but things were muddled up at Washington. I have plenty of francs so the loss of two months pay will make no difference.

You need not worry about moving. Of course Kansas City is a "good place to live in," but where you are, home is.

Tell Harry Sheskin and Miss Boggess that I shall write (so often have I said that!), and that there is not a day that I do not think of them.

I put that clipping from the "Sanskrit" in my pocket book, and shall keep it, for I have always believed the sentiment it expresses. The pine-trees you sent were indeed familiar.

I shall inclose [*sic*] several verses for Grace, and she may find them a bit more creditable than the last.

It was so dear (allow me to use a slushy term peculiar to the fair sex) of Connie to send me the book through the English girl. I thank you.

With love, Hubert

P.S. I have received Connie's of Aug. 29, and yours of the fifth and twentieth of September. I receive two others from you between those dates but cannot find them now. (I found them – 8 and 14) (over)

P.P.S. I resumed smoking after my last report, but shall quit for good if you object. "There's a reason."

Somewhere in France
October 20, 1918

Dearest Mother: The papers certainly look encouraging. Judging from their trend, I shall be at home for school next September. However, if the prophecy is not realized, I can stand another year of it if you can.

I have not heard from Clarence since August thirtieth, but if his division [went] into action, he might have to wait for my answer. I just learned that his division was only several kilos from us two weeks ago, but it may be in Valhalla now, for all I know.

Grace's letter of September seventeenth drifted in yesterday, somewhat delayed, but still spicy.

Is Uncle Phil still in Kansas City? You told me about his writing, but I don't understand yet whether he owns that newspaper, is representing it, or merely contributing. If he owns it, I might be able to help him out a bit.

I am writing a note to Miss Boggess at the same time I am writing this, and she may accept it as a peace offering. It's brevity, however, may add fuel to her wrath.

Don't worry about me. I am in perfect health and good spirits, although I'm "jolly well fed-up." I'd be worse at home though.

Pvt Hubert W. Kelley, Co. D, 12 Engineers, (LR), Amex E.7
With love,

October 28, 1918

Dearest Mother: Yours of September 26 and October 2 received, and I was glad to get your book review. I was certainly surprised at the prominence those three were given.

Clarence was mistaken about my position. I was very close to him at one time, but am not sure where he is now.

How the blankety-blank-blank did B.H. Smith ever get to be a First Lieutenant. I know something about the war, but there are a few things I can't understand. So he was showing his uniform off at school, was he? He'll be drilling my old cadet corps pretty soon, if he keeps on developing. The poor lad will get shell-shocked if he comes over here, he was always having nervous prostration over his college exams. I mean to write to him soon (Hell is paved with good intentions) and I can tell him better than I can tell you.

Tell Harry that his "Bookman" came in yesterday's mail. Fritz got the one which came last year. Not much use in writing him. I'll be home tout de suite.

I had the letter from Miss De Pallos. We were moving when it came and hence.....I wonder if I can even redeem myself.

I am following your advice. Perhaps the muse is a delicate thing to trifle with and have "laid off" completely.

You spoke of having received two verses. You should have two other envelopes full. I sent six or eight, and you should have them by now. I shall send some others very soon. With love Hubert (over) Hubert – means he has laid off smoking.

On November 9, information was received from 2nd Army Headquarters that the expected offensive would take place on November 10. Plans were made to put two rail lines into operation across No Man's Land as soon as the offensive began. The advance, however, did not take place on November 10, and on November 11, Armistice was declared. [52]

After November 11, entirely new conditions prevailed and a large forward area for operation was opened to supply the Occupation Army in its march northward. Work commenced bringing the railroad into former enemy territory on November 16. [53]

France, November 22, 1918

Dearest Mother: I am billeted in an old room where Jerry spent his evenings two weeks ago. It is a spacious apartment in something between a beast hovel and a chateau. This was the only available room in the building, for the upstairs was demolished by a well-placed bomb, and the rest of the lower suite is littered with rubbish.

We have a very comfortable room, one of the most picturesque and pleasant billets I have enjoyed (or tolerated). Illumination is very poor, but I am doing very well with a large open fireplace and a bicycle lamp found in the one of the many salvage dumps around town. There is nothing to indicate the age of the fireplace, but it has drawn many an early nineteenth century audience to its venerable hearth stone. It cracks and blazes right merrily now, but it is the first time in four years. I can fancy some of Attila's warriors trying to coax

---

[52] Ibid., p. 174–175.
[53] Ibid., p. 182, 185.

something more than an unfriendly, dismal blue blaze out of it. We can boast of wall paper in the fire light, though I believe it wouldn't bear mention in candid daylight. One of the four thieves who live in this den has relieved the wretched sweep of the bare walls with a few things of a soothing nature, such as German rifles, Very-light pistols (of which we have an abundance) and a Bavarian and Prussian helmet, none of which are especially artistic or edifying, but they sooth [*sic*] nevertheless. (I am the proud owner of the Bavarian helmet and a Very-light pistol, both of which I mean to bring home with me. The helmet is of leather with the coat-of-arms of Bavaria, a lion and unicorn rampant on the Bavarian shield, under which is inscribed "Brave and True." High over all hangs the crown. It belongs at the bottom now.) We are well equipped with furniture too. I was sitting in a cheap café chair when I started to write, but a high-backed Louis XVI affair looked more conducive to the muse and I chose it. I can't say that it facilitates matters any but the hand carving forbids my leaning back, and I must keep busy or take the plush sofa. Our beds are inviting, to say the least. Feathers and velvet make a good soldier's bones ache. We do not find sleeping a painful operation.

The family crucifix stands on the mantle [*sic*] piece, and often the French custom, I put a rose from the garden, which survived the frost, between a martyred arm and lifted cheek, and while it lived, it added some color to our gloomy little room.

When I last went on pass, I sent a few little things made near Luneville although I bought them some miles from there. The blue handkerchief is for Connie, the others for K and G, and the pillow top for you. I bought a few little Medailles en Oria for the kids, but I mean to bring them home. They are trifles but souvenirs of Jeanne d'Arc and L'ange Pleureur. With love, Hubert

France
November 29, 1918
Dearest Ouida: It has been ages since I have written to you, but it was all I could do to give an account of myself at home. I had your last letter three days ago, and was rather startled at Jr.'s irony. "I don't suppose Hubert ever gets to see the Huns; they are going so fast." He did not mean it as I took it, as you will see from the story I am about to relate.

When our company was driven out of Tincourt in March of this year, it retired to a wretched little nest of dug-out back of Peronne until Fritz could be stopped. It was a desolate valley of chalk, the sides of which were honey-combed with dug outs. Pup-tents were pitched for the night, and we awoke next morning to find the battle raging, and our immediate evacuation urgent, when, as luck would have it, our engines were found without coal. A detail was organized hurriedly, and it was my fortune to go.

When we started toward Quinconce, below Mt. St. Quentin, we did not realize the full danger of the situation. A few shells [w]ere dropping at safe distances from the "petit chemin de fer" but we paid little heed, for two days before our little detachment had gone through a veritable hail storm of fire. When we topped the ridge overlooking the valley of Quinconce, the light field artillery was retiring to the opposite slope on which stood the shack honored by the title of "Roundhouse."

We drew up, at length, at the ammunition dump at the edge of the yards and unloaded, shovels in hand. The Germans raked the valley below us steadily, while the light field artillery of the British retired methodically. Two Hun airplanes, flying at an uncomfortably low altitude roared over our heads toward the advancing German lines. Every man in the vicinity, blessed with a fire-arm, blazed away at them, when one circled, swept down, and poured a stream of machine gun bullets at the nearest concentration, and two poor Tommies hardly fifty feet behind us, went down.

We turned to, and worked like the devil. Coal dust was in our eyes and throats, but we worked. We filled what few cars in an amazingly short time, and I boarded the last train, as a British machine gun squad, every man of which was as cool as the lion after his quarter of beef, took positions in an old line of trenches to the left of the roundhouse.

We had hardly begun to move, when we heard a shout behind us, and stopped as several Tommies brought up with two wounded on stretchers. While they were placed as comfortably as possible on the last lump load of coal, I saw the Hun coming in mass formation through the blue haze on the left of the ridge. Farther to the left the British cavalry emerged from a clump of woods. "Are those British troops yonder?" asked one of our men of a British officer. We could not identify them in the mist. "Oh, no," he said, raising his field glasses very nonchalantly. "That's Jerry." The train pulled out.

I shall never forget the panorama, which lay before us as we wound down the hill into the valley. The "eighteen-pounders" were scattered as thickly as the poppies on the Somme. The gunners were stripped to waist, bringing up the back of us. Clumsily wheeled like loathesome [sic] things, and belched back their fire. The engines under steam had gone with the rest of the company, and with only the clothes on our backs, we followed. What happened next is another story, and I am sleepy.

I saw the Hun in person come over but once, but we were going too fast, he couldn't see us.

With love Hubert

(The following appears to be part of the same or a similar letter, but there is no continuity between the pages of this section and the letter above.)

...shells in a chain. The old Sergeants sat nearby on their grizzled nags, giving directions as calmly as a history teacher. Bang! Bang! Bang! The horses reared, the gun wobbled, bumped, and was whisked away a hundred yards to a new position. Here, there, everywhere, the enemy shells struck, and a heavy geyser of rock and clods went sky-high. Shells whistled over us, the batteries before us stung our faces while our heads throbbed with the thunder and shriek of it all. Little yellow puffs burst over the valley like cotton balls, and the sickening zig-zag buzz of the shrapnel fragments sang over the valley.

There a shell struck directly in the lorry-packed road, and wheels, beams, and debris went up in smoke. Farther up on the opposite hill a shell dropped with a scream into a herd of remounts, and the horses stampeded, and some kicked and foamed in the grass.

Needless to say we got out of it. When we reached our rendezvous, the tanks...

Toward the end of November, the Twelfth entered into a trying time. The war was over, work was robbed of interest and excitement. Thoughts turned to going home.

Pass privileges were reinstituted and every man was given the opportunity of a week's leave to Aix les Bains, Grenoble, or some other leave center.

Each post built a theatre where YMCA troupes and other entertainment groups could perform. Motion picture equipment was obtained so each company could have a film showing every week. [54]

---

[54] Ibid., p. 194.

Suzemont, France
December 1, 1918

Dear Father: Perhaps, you will find the absence of "Somewhere" rather startling, but no doubt you have already read of the modification of censorship rules. We are handling the German light-gauge railway at Suzemont near Conflans. Conflans, as you may have learned from the American's last communiqués, is a very important railway center. At the end, our artillery dominated the heights overlooking that city, but fortunately, the signing of the armistice saved it from destruction. Suzemont together with an adjoining village, Hannonville, forms a compact billeting center, which the Germans used for their troops. It is on the Metz-Verdun road some thirty-two kilos from one and thirty-six from the other. The Lorraine border is about twelve kilos to the east. I was across the border last week, over the old battle ground of Mars-la-Tour of the Franco-Prussian war, and into the Lorrainian village of Dionville.

We occupied this village about five days after the German evacuation – that is, on the eighteenth of November but I saw a calendar in an office here bearing a notation made the seventeenth of the month. Whether the memorandum was to be referred to on that date, or whether it was written on the seventeenth, I do not know. The context would imply the former, since it dealt with something to be mentioned to the officer's company. In my call-book (I am calling crews) I found a German note headed "11-13-18," and addressed "Dear Enemy." It was an expression of joy at the fact the war was over.

I suppose you would like to know something of our travels aside from the experiences in this country. It would be unkind to write a history – the censor still exists –but I can give you our route to our present location.

We landed at Bologne-sur-Mer via Halifax N.S., Liverpool, Borden, London, and South Hampton. We lay in a rest camp three days, went to Roisel, Montigny Farm, and then our company was detached and assigned to Tincourt, where we operated British narrow gauge until the retreat of March. We stayed at Tincourt about thirty-six hours after the push started.

I went up beyond Villers Faucon on a track detail of some sixteen men to repair the track as fast as Fritz blew it up. We were in the very worst of it all day, with little chance of getting out alive. I remember one particularly tight place we squeezed out of. Fritz had torn a crater through our rails and ballast, at "CY nine" and we repaired the damage while an ammunition dump went up in flames in our very faces, and shells dropped in salvos of five or six about the place. As we worked, the pioneer engineers dug the next line of trenches behind us. But I promised not to write a history.

From Tincourt we retired to Hem behind Peronne, then to the crossroads near Wiencourt, thence to Combles, Valheureux, and an unnamed field before Albert. At Terramesnil near Doullens and Val de Maison we dug a reserve line of trenches, working in conjunction with the Hindus and Chinese, and then to Woirel we marched via Flixecourt. We stayed there working on broad-gauge construction from Oisemont to Airaines till late in July when we left the British, and joined he American forces at Baccarat on the Moselle *(arriving July 27)*. You probably know that I went to Luneville on leave. We were assigned to light-gauge construction near the front, where we worked at night. *(They were ordered by the newly arrived American division's commanding general not to work at all during the day.)* We were seldom bothered there, except at about ten in the evening when Jerry made his nightly excursion to Baccarat. He had [a] little habit of dropping illuminating bombs right when our shovels were hot, and we were forced to flatten on the cold ground.

At the beginning of the final preparations at Saint-Mihiel, we were ordered to Sorcy-sur-Meuse, to operate to the line and follow the advance. I was detached to Neuf Etang (nine pools) on a section detail, and saw the bombardment of Mt. Sec, the commanding observation hill held by the Germans. The artillery changed its color from green to clay before the night, when I went to Roulecourt on a wrecking gang. I returned to Sorcy as a telephone operator and was orderly in the superintendent's office when we left to come into this country. I hope our next move is homewards.

On the whole, we have had good luck. We.... *(Parts of this paragraph are illegible.)* Shall fire before Cam.... year ago yesterday. All ...of fire and brimstone too in march on the Somme, and saw the outer edges of the crushing of the St. Mihiel Salient. The next big event will be the sight of the "Statue of Liberty." God grant that it be soon. With love, Hubert

Suzemont, France
December 10, 1918
Dearest Mother: It seems as if I had not written you for a year, time drags so slowly. This town is dead, although the civilians are returning, but they are like ghosts. They say little, and move about so forlornly that they seem hardly human. The town is dead.

I moved my billet from the silent gray house across the street to the cozy little back room of this place. There is more life in this house. One has a sense of companionship here – and the house has an atmosphere of occupation. Over there I could not overcome the dismal sense of loneliness which the utter emptiness of the great cluttered rooms invariably produced. No matter how big a fire we built. Or how boisterous our talk, the light flickered in spacious corners and high, scarred walls, and our laugh echoed from distant rooms or long, gloomy hallways.

The civilians occupied the place two days ago. I came in at evening to find everyone gone, and an old woman (old as the house, she seemed) peering about the gloomy rooms with a candle held above her head. The poor old soul was glad to see me, told me leave what I could not carry until the next day, and led me away on a tour of inspection. She led me to the cupboard, opened the door to the empty shelves, and told me that the Boche had taken all. She told me how many plates, glasses, and knives and forks he had taken; how many dresses had gone for plunder, and how he had broken up her furniture for firewood. She fumbled about the trash on the floor, musing on fragments of china, on buttons, and letters, and snarled like an animal when she found fresh evidences of the Germans' destructiveness.

It was a wet, miserable evening, and the troops were marching past in the mud on the sludgy road, and I was alone in the house with that old wrinkled woman. The rats squealed and scampered through the littered rooms, and the candle light gleamed on the wet stones in the hall-way. I could not help thinking of home. What a contrast! Soft-carpeted floors, deep cushions, clear, steady lights, and the gleam in darkened rooms on polished oak and red mahogany! Starched curtains, clean sheets on light springy beds, white dresses, the benediction of all-pervading warmth, running water! Happy voices, music, books, and children! O, one cannot realize what it all means until he has seen what we see, and live amidst. Of course you know what it all means, for you have seen the rough edges of life. But the children do not know.

But enough of this sermon. It is too depressing. We are looking forward to the Spring, for we expect to blow in with the spring flowers. Home! Home! Home! We talk and think of nothing else, but it is not good for us. We do it nevertheless.

I am enclosing some souvenirs, which I hope may reach you safely. The German "War Bond" is for Grace, and the "Iron Cross" is for Kathleen. She is the youngest, and can pass it down as an heirloom to the little Kathleens. I believe it will reach you safely. With love, Hubert

P.S. The cross was awarded to an officer and it is very valuable.

Suzemont

December 15, 1918

Dear Mother: I am sending you a picture taken in front of our old office at Sorcy-sur-Meuse. We made a feeble attempt at appearing warlike but succeeded only in looking top-heavy.

You may find some of these postals interesting. I made pilgrimage to Rezonville in the rain to get them, and studied the originals as I passed them on the road. The French National Monument is at the crossroads before Mare-la-Tour. The most interesting feature of it, perhaps, is the hideous spectacle in the vault below it. All of the bones of the soldiers killed around Mare-la-Tour during the Franco-Prussian war are piled in open niches around the cavern. One has access to it by an iron trap door opening to a short steep flight of steps. It is dark and foul below, and the water stands an inch deep on the floor. Some of the bones have slid from their orderly piles to float on the stagnant pool.

The monument to the German regiments from Alvensleben has been mutilated ludicrously by the occupying army. Some one has put a nose-bag for stock feeding over the face of the standing Hun, while the kneeling soldier has yielded half of his ready rifle to a hack-saw. The uplifted sword of the former now flies a tattered tri-color.

The other cards bear only a common interest. The grand entrance into Metz is a very recent photograph.

Your letter of the thirteenth and Connie's of the twenty-third came day before yesterday. I received one from Clarence at the same time. I do not suppose I can see him, unless we go to the coast, which is very unlikely before Spring. He will probably be gone by that time.

Harry wrote me from barracks about the middle of October, and his letter just arrived along with a bundle of magazines. He should be mustered out by this time. Tell him I have written, and I shall write again as soon as things settle. It's all I can do to keep in touch with you, and cope with the idleness and the miserable uncertainty of the times. I am wearing a beautiful ring bearing the double cross of Lorraine surrounded by Lorrainian thistles, which I mean to bring home with me. I got it for Harry, for he appreciates anything of that kind as few people do. Give him my love and tell him I'll drift in with the Spring.

If you do not get the coupon I sent you for the Christmas box on time, don't worry, because we get along very well, and need very little. I appreciate a big letter from you or the kids more than I care for anything else you could send.

I haven't written to Papa as often as I should, perhaps, but I always try to make my letters do for the family. I hope his health was not impaired by the malaria, and that he is well completely. If he doesn't go south again, I shan't worry.

The aviator should be out of service now. His high life was short, but he shouldn't be bothered. Of course Connie will wait till I get home. I have a chronic distaste for aviators – I have dodged too many of them – and I want to be in on the big works, and see one aviator take the hardest fall he ever experienced. School teachers are as uncertain as air currents.

I saw one aviator get his last New Year's Day at Tincourt. The machine gun across the road made his plane look like a sieve. Lucky that Maurice didn't get across. (This is to raise Connie's morale.)

With love, Hubert

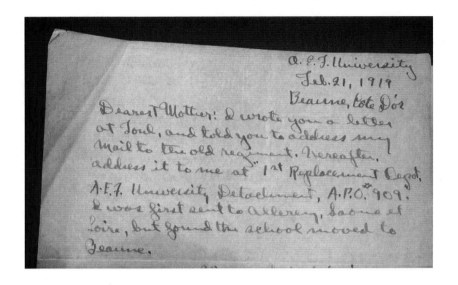

Letters from 1919

January 11, 1919

Dear Sis: I have had the book for several weeks, and I almost forgot to acknowledge it. After thanking the second member of the relay, it completely slipped my mind, until you mentioned it the other day.

We are still at Sorcy-la-Gare and working as if the war had not finished. We are given a few injections of propaganda occasionally, and almost believe we are going home the middle of next month, so that morale drags along with a sick sort of anticipation toward the goal.

I feel rather groggy today, and the inspiration cannot cope with the incentive to write. I made a pilgrimage to a French canteen this morning, and bought some French cheese, and between the weight of it and the recollections of the fumes I inhaled while eating it, I am almost incapacitated.

Miss Boggess's Sergeant wandered over here the other day, and we became acquainted. I was so busy calling crews, I had little time to talk, so after setting our dates of departure from this "sacred" soil, he left. I may meet him again, for he is with a supply train at Commercy. He seems to be a decent sort of a chap.

I never did get to see Clarence, and probably will not see him until I get back. He should be on his way home now. Did you know I haven't seen a soul I knew in the States since I came to France?

I am enclosing some cards I found in my "blue-bag." Some of them I brought down from the Somme. You may have copies of them at home. The others I bought near Metz in Lorraine, when we were camped at Sugemont-sur-Yrou.

By the time you receive this letter, we hope to have some definite news. The morale dropped several times when it was rumored we were going to Russia, and when, on another occasion, someone said we had six months more work laid out for us. Not that I discredit the last entirely, but the sun has popped out again, and we are looking forward to the fifteenth of next month. I am sure I will be back in time to vote against the prospective candidate for President on the Republican ticket.

With love, Hubert

Poem (pencil-written, no attribution or date)

There was a time when every shrub and tree
Seemed incarnate divinity.
When every flower effused an aureole
From Nature's all-pervading soul;

When moonlight, soft as God's benignant gaze,
And sunlight's warm effulgent blaze
Imparted, as they permeated me,
The joy of trembling ecstasy.

The diapasow [*sic*] of the shades and sounds,
The ambient beauty that abounds
Inspired my spirit with divine delight
Till surfeits seared me like a blight.

~~~~~~~~

The early part of 1919 was spent in the salvage of ammunition and engineering materials. Early figures show a high of 5,112 tons on January 3 with amounts lessening at the end of the month. Gradually the operation of the broad-gauge lines were turned over to either the French or the 22nd Engineers.[55]

---

[55] Ibid., p. 199ff.

Dijon

January 16, 1919

Dear Mother: I am on my way to Grenoble, about fifty miles from the Italian frontier, opposite Turin. I had a leave sooner than I expected, and am half finished with my journey now.

It is after mid-night but I am not tired. I caught a wink of sleep on the car I came here on. This rest-room is warm, there is plenty of paper, hence, this letter.

I shall write again when I reach my destination, so don't worry over terseness of this "missive" or, as the Duchess says, "this missile."

Our officers warned us to take care of ourselves, for [they] said we are to return to God's country shortly after the leave is up. Don't depend on O.D. propaganda, but I almost believe Captain McGeehan, whom I met at Headquarters. "We leave about the fifteenth of February," he said. With love, Hubert

January 19

Dearest Mother: You should have received my letter from Dijon by this time, and you may not be surprised to know that I am at Uriage-les-bains near Grenoble. Grenoble, as you may see on the map, is in the Department of Isere on the river Isere, which is a tributary of the Rhone. We are about one hundred miles from the borders of Italy, and some few miles more from the Mediterranean Sea.

The first settlement on the site of the present city of Grenoble was made as early as five hundred years before Christ. I believe it was founded by the Sabiani, a Gaelic tribe. Gratian, a Roman emperor, surrounded the town several hundred years after its settlement, and founded a new city called Gratianopolis, with the Gaelic city as a nucleus. The French name comes from the Roman.

Uriage is nested at the end of a valley in the Occidental Alps, at the edge of a range known as the Cotienne, I think.

Mountains wall us in here. Above the lower pine-covered ridges rise the peaks and distant ridges. On one hand Mount Colombe gleams above the fleecy clouds which wreathe its shoulders. The people here call it the Great White Mountain. At this time of the year it is a wondrous upheaval of dazzling white and splendor. Shoulder to shoulder stand its comrades, Leperlay and the Mountain of the Great Winds (Gran de Vents). They are rugged, even ___, and bear their snow in drifts, while cold rocks protrude naked from the mantles.

The government has done remarkably well here. It has chartered all the hotels of the summer resort for enlisted men on leave. Unlike my Paris trip last year, everything is furnished – transportation, meals, and room. Newby and I have a veritable palace in the Hotel Monnet, and all for three service chevrons.

We have a medieval castle perched on a mound about our back window. It is a real stronghold of romance, with walls at its base encircling it, turrets, spires, and a hostelry at its entrance. One can almost fancy an Italian knight leading his horse up the steep winding path which leads from the valley to the portals, when he looks down from a higher eminence. We climbed to it and above yesterday, and drank milk at a farmer's house away up in the mountains. The valley lay in haze below us, and a great free expanse of cold blue nothing stretched from where we sat to the snow-capped, pine coated peaks and ranges beyond. Drinking milk in the Alps is quite an experience.

Forgive these frequent digressions, but I have so much to tell, and am so anxious to get this letter off my mind, that I cannot be very systematic.

Newby and I hired "bicyclettes" this afternoon and went for a spin down the valley, and were so rewarded by the unusual experiment that we shall repeat.

I am writing in the Y.M.C.A. It has beautiful quarters here – everything a sensible man could ask for. The Theatre in the building would do the best cinema in Kansas City justice. There is a library, billiard room, and canteen for privates, not to mention the dancing hall and café.

I shall write again before I leave. I have no inclination to write, for I expect to be home soon. Our officers told us, before we left, to take good care of ourselves, for we were to return next month, and could not return with disease of any kind. With love, Hubert

Sorcy-la-Gare
January 29, 1919

Dearest Mother: On my way to Uriage, I wrote to Clarence without a thought that he could possibly meet me there. He arrived in Uriage from Grenoble on the tram way as I was leaving. At the Y.M.C.A. he found my name in the register, found I had gone to Grenoble, and followed me.

Our Sergeant was distributing some bread amongst us, and Clarence heard him call my name from the platform of the depot, boarded the train, and dragged me out. I talked to him about thirty minutes but we could never get down to business. It was probably my fault. I was too upset to talk coherently. I was Paris bound, headed for Lyon, where I was to change for the P.L.&M., but while I talked to Clarence, I didn't know where I was. It all seemed like a dream, although things have cleared up wonderfully since I came here.

He seemed to be in the best trim, his spirit was high, and altogether he seemed like Clarence at home. He seemed to be so much smaller to me – completely out of proportion to what I fancied him, but it is possibly because I have grown so much myself. You should have heard from him by this time, and get the other side of it. I hope he has a clearer side than I have given you. I was so upset at seeing him as unexpectedly as I did, that it is all hazy to me.

I found your Christmas letter, Connie's of the twenty-seventh, and Kathleen's "oration" on the Iron Cross I sent when I returned. With love, Hubert

P.S. Why has Papa quit writing? Clarence was rather worried.

(The story was told by Hubert's eldest son, HWK Jr., that after his grandfather, John M. Kelley, finished work in the shipyard in New Orleans as a Master Machinist, he received a good bonus check. He woke up penniless in Illinois with a couple of months unaccounted for. He was a 32nd Degree Mason, and earlier in life had been a blacksmith and a hardware salesman.)

Sorcy-la-Gare
February 5, 1919
Dearest Mother: Your letter of Jan. 17 just arrived. It narrowly escaped passing me on the sea, for the regiment is mobilizing shortly. We hope to be up and away by the first of the month. I was foolish enough to put my name in application for examination for admission into West Point, and if, by chance, the regiment should sail before the date set for the examination, and the examination should be held on French soil, I might be ordered to remain. But I should return immediately as a casual. Don't take this seriously. It is but a supposition.

I know Clarence Woodbury very well. His company moved here to the rail-head to-day. It is strange you did not know we were great friends. I thought I had mentioned him before.

(In March 1959, Clarence Woodbury, who became a reporter for the New York Daily News, wrote "They Fought With Picks and Shovels," an article on the battle in which many of the 11th Engineers were killed when, unarmed except for shovels, they were attacked by the enemy, and he quoted HWK's poem on the incident. It was published in the American Legion Magazine. See notes following November 26, 1917.)

Tell Grace her letter in reply to the bond came through. K. & G. mustn't think I shall be led around like a monkey when I get back. I am to be a retired soldier – a peaceful veteran, and the only speeches I mean to make will be made at mine own fireside. I may get me a cane, and sit on a park bench on sunny days. If I see a Civil War veteran on his front porch, I shall insist, forcibly if necessary, that he is a fraud, and knows nothing at all about war.

Don't build up too many hopes on my return, for the army is heartless. It wrecks hopes and homes and never apologizes. With love, Hubert

Toul

February 12

Dearest Mother: I am here at Toul for the night en route to Allerey, Saone et Loire, below Dijon. I shall join my new unit there, the 1st Replacement Depot Battalion.

The Twelfth is leaving next week for the States, and I was transferred at the last minute. My prophecy is fulfilled. My application for examination for entrance to West Point was answered by a transfer. This involves my staying on French soil until March eighteenth at least. Of course matters could be much worse. I should not have transferred on my own accord, but after my application, I was given no option.

I am to be sent to school at Allerey, preparation to taking the examination, so I am losing no valuable time. Make the most of it as I am doing. C'est la guerre! I may be home soon.

Address all my mail to the Twelfth, until I give you my permanent address – With love, Hubert

P.S. I am writing on my hucksac and am doing a miserable job.

At the beginning of 1919, Sorcy-la-Gare was picked as the embarkation point, and all companies of the 12th Engineers were assembled there. On February 28, orders were issued to move the Twelfth to Bordeaux, and three days later, 60 American boxcars were placed at Sorcy-la-Gare and loading began. Early in February, Hubert had departed for the school where he would prepare for the West Point entrance exam.)[56]

---

[56] Ibid., p. 214.

Undated, some page(s) missing. Probably February 1919

I learned a few things while I was in school, and found I knew more about geometry than I ever suspected – thanks to Miss Harriman.

There are very few in the University wearing three service chevrons. I have seen only three or four. I do not think that many of the first thirty-thousand are left. They are either above American soil or under French. I get my fourth gold chevron in July, but I think the dog Connie put in my Christmas package will save me. I wear it around my neck, for an old Frenchman I met on the Lyon train (he was discharged and returning to his home in Jerusalem) told me it was my fetish.

Give my love to all, but keep the most for yourself – Hubert

Beaune, Cote D'or
February 21, 1919

Dearest Mother: I wrote you a letter at Toul, and told you to address my mail to the old regiment. Hereafter, address it to me a[t] "1st Replacement Depot, A.E. F. University Detachment, A.P.O #909." I was first sent to Allerey, Saone et Loire, but found the school moved to Beaune.

We are billeted in an evacuated hospital barracks with cement floors and tile walls. We use hospital beds and mattresses and were issued extra blankets. This is the first time in my army career in France that I have had a clean, warm place to sleep. We have an excellent kitchen, and we are promised more rations.

There are about two hundred men in our detachment. I believe that every State in the country is represented in our hut alone, while almost every unit of any importance in France has candidates here.

A course of academic studies is furnished us by Y.M.C.A. instructors picked from the faculties of the American colleges. Our English teacher was the head of the department of English in the Nebraska University before he came in the service. He is very much like Mr. Smith, except he permits smoking between recitations. Our books are furnished by the government. They are very elementary, but, to be candid, I find the subject matter absolutely foreign. I am taking Algebra and Geometry again, and recognize a few old enemies among the equations and theorems. If I can get myself down to serious studying, I might get something out of the course. It lasts till March eighteenth, when we take the West Point examination.

I really have no desire to pass it, except for the satisfaction personally. In the first place, a cadet, upon entering, must sign up for eight years in the army. I would serve in no army in time of peace. In the second place, mathematics are emphasized, and I refuse to be a mathematician. In the next place, I want to go home, and stay home for a while, and West Point makes no allowance for furlough until the third year, with the possible exception of Christmas. Some may think you must take a boy from home to make a man of him, but the right kind of a home is the most refining place in the world.

With love, Hubert

P.S. I am pretty sure I shall be home by the first of April. In the mean time I shall make the best of compulsory education.

Beaune, France
March 2, 1919

Dearest Mother: I had an opportunity to transfer back to the "Twelfth" and took it. I am not in the "A.E.F. University Service Battalion, Third Company, Pioneer." My application for transfer has been approved and forwarded and I am awaiting developments. Of course, things have not come as they might [but] I am sure to be home eventually. Please don't take the situation seriously.

My mail will undoubtedly be delayed, for I have been moving so much lately that the post office cannot keep up. Since I came here, I have received no mail, but I shall get a sack full when it arrives, I am sure.

I am in the best of health, in comfortable barracks, and am very well contented with the way things are turning. *(Letter ends.)*

Tours, France
March 18, 1919

Dearest Mother: My last letter had a rather discouraging color scheme, but my "fetish" has adjusted things, and I am on my way to Bordeaux, the port of embarkation. My regiment has been there several weeks awaiting shipment, and I do not suppose I shall have to wait long before sailing.

I thought for a while that I was due for nine months more in France with the Service Battalion, but things must turn out right. So, at last, the old, broken-down veteran is on the trail of the fatted calf.

But remember, I may lose the "fetish" so let not thy hopes soar too high.

I leave Tours for the port at about midnight.

With love to all, I am your son, Hubert

Bordeaux, France
April 3, 1919

Dearest Mother: At last I am deloused, equipped and awaiting transportation. How long I must wait, I do not know, but I am hopeful enough to believe that I shall sail April seas.

I am with the regiment again and you may rest assured that I shall not leave it again very soon. I found it at La Lustre some thirty kilometers from Bordeaux, and marched with it to the embarkation camp.

I do not know whether the regiment will go to St. Louis or not. We may be sent to demobilization camps upon arrival in New York. According to the papers here, men are to be discharged forty-eight hours after entering demobilization camps.

I mean to go to work as soon as possible on my return, and attend night school until the fall term at Poly opens. If I can learn stenography I will have gained a mechanical foundation for journalistic work.

I am afraid Clarence will have to weather another winter over here, but, from what I can learn, the army of occupation is not having a bad time of it.

I saw in the "Herald" that the "79th F.A." staged a performance at 'Colombey-les-belles,' (wherever that is) so Clarence should be somewhere near there.

I took the pneumonia shot a week ago, so don't worry about the influenza. There are several million combatant bugs doing close order drill in my arteries.

Don't get too anxious. I'll drift in a few weeks behind this letter. With love, Hubert P.S. These pens are impossible.

Embarkation finally came on April 13, 1919, and the Cape May departed by 5:50 p.m. down the Gironde River. They encountered terrible weather but finally set out into the Bay of Biscay, where everyone was incredibly seasick for several days. On the night of April 26, the lights of Coney Island were sighted, and the next morning the Cape May dropped anchor in the lower harbor of New York. A huge welcome was waiting. The largest detachment, containing men from Missouri, Kansas, and eastern Illinois, some six hundred men and officers, were routed through St. Louis on their way to Camp Funston for discharge.[57]

---

[57] Ibid., p. 223.

USS *Cape May*

At Sea, April 24, 1919 [Postcard]

This will be mailed on landing. Seven hundred miles from U.S.A. Heavy
fog – Hubert

Sent to Mrs. J.M. Kelley, 3119 E. 30th St, Kansas City, MO.

Other letters sent to:

Mr. JM Kelley

3203 College St.

Kansas City, MO

Headquarters: 12h Engineers LR, Co. D

Pvt 1 Cl Hubert W. Kelly [*sic*]

Camp Upton, NY May 5, 1919

Has permission to be absent from his station and duties with authority to
visit New York City from 10Pm May 5th until 700 AM May 8th 1919.

Approved by order of Col Laird, Cl Johnson Capt Eugin. US Regular Army
Recruit Station, Camp Upton, NY.

Undated Letter Fragments

from 1918, before and after the Armistice

1. These are great days. The moon comes up with a clear conscience, and
she has regained some of her queenly beauty. For four years France has not
dared to look her square in the face, for fear some low-flying Boche would
perforate her own visage with machine gun bullets. At night some of the boys
go out in the fields and shoot star lights full in moon light to demonstrate their
fearlessness. My way was lit by Verey-lights all the road home. They shed a
wonderful blue light for a few seconds while misty fields glimmer and black
shadows rush for cover.

I suppose you wonder when the boys will come home. So do the boys. I
fear Clarence will stay longest, but strange things happen. The last I heard of
him, he was on the coast in a "training".....

2. Connie's and Kathleen's letters came with yours up to the last of October. Your pictures were great. The best picture I ever had of Connie came when we were in the woods. The last one was good though. Send me a good one of Kathleen. The picture of Maurice and Grace was one of the best pictures of its kind I ever saw.

I am inclosing [*sic*] a picture of one of our old offices; with two or three rookies in.....

3. ...looked for. We see shells fall. In fact, I saw the Germans bombard a pathetic pile of ruins with "eight-point-twos" not long ago. Just to-day I saw an airplane fall in flames after an air battle.

I have never told you that I was among the first contingent of foreign troops under arms to march through London since William the Conqueror overcame Harold at the battle of Hastings in 1066. I saw the King and Queen, and candidly say that I was not impressed with the royalty. I do not stand for monarchy, even though it be a figurehead. I would have told you sooner about this trip, but was afraid of censorship; I understand that.....

4. Well, I must au revoir for the present. I hope this reaches you uncensored. When you receive this I shall be nineteen, for, as you may remember, it thundered on September 8, 1899. (Incidentally, I picked up a French newspaper in a gutted grave-yard, dated March – 1889. I read some of it. I shall keep it for a souvenir – maybe.

This letter is too long already – so must close on behalf of the censor. Give my love to all – including "ye faculty." As ever, your son, Hubert

5. I received several "K.C. Stars" the last mail and have read, with some satisfaction the "Star's" attack on the conditions prevailing at Funston. It is outrageous that such inefficiency as that is tolerated.

I understand from the letters I have had from home that you are reading my mail second-handed. I prefer to unwind my thoughts in the letters I write home. I intended that they be passed around to the detached part of the family. You know yourself that it is a deuce of a bore to write, repeat, and restate. I know you understand, and that you will not be too hard on me for not writing more to you.

I hope you are in good health, and that you are taking care... *(Letter ends.)*

Other poems by H.W. Kelley about the war

On the Way to Bois Foret
Published by the *Kansas City Star*, date unknown

On the way to Bois Foret,
When the morning glimmered gray,
Frosty lipped the fallen lay
On the way to Bois Foret.

Crumpled in the crisp, gray grass,
Still they lay, the fallen dead;
Yet they seemed to hear us pass,
And we thought their voices said,
Speaking in the columns tread,

"Yesterday our blood was bold,
As we marched to Bois Foret,
Now we lie stiff, lifeless clay,
Stricken still, and we are cold.
We are cold, as here we lie,
Frosty face to steely sky.

Stinging numb, the hard wind blows
Memories of bitter snows.
Cold the moon's thin, crescent rim
Hangs above you creaking limb;
Cold the morning star which still
Stares with eye of silver chill.
Yesterday our blood was bold;
Now our hearts are cold, are cold.

Up the way to Bois Foret
Stopped we where the fallen lay,
Dropped our packs, and gently spread
Things we needed o'er the dead,
Though we knew unconscious clay

Could not know we passed that way.
Cold and rain might work us harm,
But we left the fallen warm.

~~~~~~~~

The Ballad of the Engineer
1917

A hogger on the C&A, the Wabash, or the Santa Fe,
Or Burlington I've heard some say,
Passed 8th and Main one fateful day,
And Shaw, or someone green as grass, beheld the noble hoghead pass,
And said "There goes a silly ass," then put upon the shiny glass,
That gaudy, glaring, gripping sign "Enlist to run the CY Line."

This patriotic engineer had heard, as others often hear,
That war had lately been declared, by Shaw, or maybe Major Laird,
And since he was out on a spree, with views on World Democracy,
He turned, and pushed the door aside, walked to the desk with w[o]bbling stride,
And said "Well, Captain, here I am, to engineer for Uncle Sam.
Just give me sleep and three square meals; a monkey stove on engine wheels
A coalcar full of crisp hardtack, and if you'll clear the CY track,
I'll drive 'er down to 'ell and back."

"I'll drive to Strasbourg, or Cologne, I'll ride around the Kaiser's throne
I'll fill his mustache full of soot, and steam out Hindenburg to boot."

"That's very well, brave engineer," the Captain said with half a sneer,
"Your army chances will be better, when you show me your service letter."
It did not take him long to show, he'd worked from Maine to Mexico,
And so he signed his signature, and swore an oath to make it sure.

To make a weary story short, this engineer sailed into port,

With porridge dripping from his jaws, and shreds of "Bully" in his claws,
And landed "Somewhere in France," to eat hardtack and gandy-dance.

And there he lives unto this day, with thirty dollars for his pay.
Profanity is on his lips, his pockets full of poker chips.
His shirt is wriggling with the fleas, the crabs, and Belgian refugees.
He swings the pick and wields the spade, and sweats but tea and cold lime-ade.
He sighs and digs, and digs and sighs, and carries rails and railroad ties.

The moral is – Don't volunteer to be an Army engineer.
For if they get you out in France, they'll surely make you gandy-dance.

The Ravings of the Rum Hound
1917

I've swallowed all the wines that flow,
From Burgundy to red Bordeaux,
I've gurgled gin and lager beer,
And drinks that stimulate and cheer,
I've funneled absinthe, strong and green,
And drinks that make you wild and mean,
I've swallowed all that man has brewed,
But none of them has left me stewed.

But when I came [to] bloody France,
To do my bit and take my chance,
I found a liquor new to me,
'Twould make a rabbit climb a tree,
'Twould make a timid kitten roar,
'Twould send the Dove of Peace to War,
And so one black and moonless night
I went to see why "Tommies" fight,
And bought for thirty francs, I think,
A jug of British Rum to drink.

I've gurgled whiskey, wine, and gin,
But never will I drink again;
Of all the drinks I've ever swilled,
That man's concocted or distilled,
That man has filtered, man has brewed,
The one that left me shot and stewed,
That wrecked me, burnt me, knocked me dead,
That dazed me, crazed me, cracked my head,
Was that infernal hellish slop,
That sends a "Tommie" o'er the top.

I think that rum is made of fire,
Of nine-point two's, and rusty wire,
Of shrapnel, bombs and oily arms,
Of hardtack, mines, and gas alarms,
Of guts, and guns, and picks and spades,
Of bayonets and hand grenades,
Of blood and thunder, shot and shell,
All boiled and bottled up in Hell.

I took a drink, another still,
I had a fever, then a chill,
My head it whirled, my knees they shook,
And two drinks were all I took,
I staggered homeward through the night,
And now I know why "Tommies" fight.
I reached my hut, and found my bunk;
O Lord, but I was crazy drunk.

The boys sat up and looked around,
And called me "Stew"and "Damned Rum Hound,"
"Get down," I yelled, "Get down in bed,
I'll raise a barrage 'round your head."
And then I took a fireman's role,
And filled the Sibley full of coal.

Postwar Poem

The Warrior Passes
(On Woodrow Wilson's passing,
The Kansas City Journal Post, February 1924)

In S Street trod the fantom guard—
 The men of Argonne—men of Aisne
Who battled well and battled hard
 And, sorely wounded, died in vain.
Forgotten dead were on parade—
 A mangled crew, if men would know—
But still with faces undismayed,
 They marched with majesty and, lo,

On S Street to the rendezvous—
 The darkened house—they came at last:
The sergeant silently withdrew—
 The lipless bugler shrilled a blast;
The President! The gallant call
 Startled the shadows with its flame,
And from the doorway, gaunt and tall,
 The President—the Chieftain came!

Martyred and old, the Chieftain came
 To meet the warrior guard of death.
His brow was hurt, his body lame;
 His heart was still and still his breath.
His greatness, like a shining cloak,
 Obscured his broken form and bent;
The ghastly sergeant wheeled and spoke,
 And rifles mounted to "Present!"

In S Street—in the street of grief—
 The deathly guard of honor trod,
Bearing the spirit of their Chief
 Into the cabinet of God.
How different another day!

The thundering cheers that would not cease!
When glittering Paris thronged the way
  Into the rendezvous of peace!

They marched away—the guard of death—
  Silent and grim behind the Great;
And phantom Youth without a breath
  Whispered unto his mangled mate,
"What is the thing about his face
  "That makes me dream of something dim—
"A crucifix at some torn place
  "And the shell-scarred face of Him."

G. H. Q.
AMERICAN EXPEDITIONARY FORCES,

GENERAL ORDERS]
No. 38-A. }

FRANCE, *February 28, 1919.*

MY FELLOW SOLDIERS:

Now that your service with the American Expeditionary Forces is about to terminate, I can not let you go without a personal word. At the call to arms, the patriotic young manhood of America eagerly responded and became the formidable army whose decisive victories testify to its efficiency and its valor. With the support of the nation firmly united to defend the cause of liberty, our army has executed the will of the people with resolute purpose. Our democracy has been tested, and the forces of autocracy have been defeated. To the glory of the citizen-soldier, our troops have faithfully fulfilled their trust, and in a succession of brilliant offensives have overcome the menace to our civilization.

As an individual, your part in the world war has been an important one in the sum total of our achievements. Whether keeping lonely vigil in the trenches, or gallantly storming the enemy's stronghold; whether enduring monotonous drudgery at the rear, or sustaining the fighting line at the front, each has bravely and efficiently played his part. By willing sacrifice of personal rights; by cheerful endurance of hardship and privation; by vigor, strength and indomitable will, made effective by thorough organization and cordial co-operation, you inspired the war-worn Allies with new life and turned the tide of threatened defeat into overwhelming victory.

With a consecrated devotion to duty and a will to conquer, you have loyally served your country. By your exemplary conduct a standard has been established and maintained never before attained by any army. With mind and body as clean and strong as the decisive blows you delivered against the foe, you are soon to return to the pursuits of peace. In leaving the scenes of your victories, may I ask that you carry home your high ideals and continue to live as you have served—an honor to the principles for which you have fought and to the fallen comrades you leave behind.

It is with pride in our success that I extend to you my sincere thanks for your splendid service to the army and to the nation.

Faithfully,

John J. Pershing

Commander in Chief.

OFFICIAL:
ROBERT C. DAVIS,
Adjutant General.

Copy furnished to ____ Hubert W. Kelley., Private 1cl.

[signature]

Capt., Engrs., USA

Company D, 12th Engineers (LR).

A Memory of Amiens

Kansas City Star, Sunday, March 29, 1931

I do not keep things—mementos, I mean. I have always believed that everything I ever saw or touched or felt in any way was kept for me—inside. Perhaps that is not true, but it seems to me that I can turn into myself, grope down into the dark pool of forgotten things and recover sensations I thought I had lost. But no matter—

I have kept one thing—a dim, gray photograph of a stone cherub—"L'Ange Pleureur," it was called, "The Weeping Angel." I framed it a few years ago and hung it on my wall. Certainly it adds nothing to the beauty of the room, but it gives me a feeling whenever I look at it, a feeling I need not grope for—a poignant sense of loss. I cannot exactly explain it. There is nothing of despair in my feeling about that picture. It is saddening, but it fills me with a strange, formless hope. The walls around me become insubstantial, the easy chair by the fire becomes a stone that I rest upon in the wilderness.

I saw the weeping angel for the last time thirteen years ago—in March, it was, this month. It sat on a shelf of marble in a gloomy recess of the vast and caverned Cathedral of the Beautiful God in Amiens. I had discovered the little statue there a year before. I had no gods then, so needing one, I chose this forlorn figure of medieval stone. It was just a whim, a passing whim. I laughed about it.

But always when I went to Amiens from the front on a weekend holiday, I walked straightway to the cathedral to see my sad cherub. One of its hands rested on an hour glass, the other upon a skull. Its head was bowed. Oh, time and death! I stood there for a little while in the gloom and went away.

It was just a whim, I say. After my whimsical pilgrimage I walked down the dewy cobblestones of the main street, between tinted facades, looking for my wineshop, the only one that opened at dawn.

Perhaps Amiens is drab to the tourist. But to me, on my occasional weekend leaves from the front that year, it seemed to be the loveliest city on earth. I always left the front at midnight on a boxcar and rode into the station at the first pink of morning, sleepless but happy as a lark.

The mounded dug-outs, the gray shacks and sandbags, the torn brown earth and rusty wire, the foundations of fallen villages, the dreary, muddy soldiers, the smoke and rumble—they were behind me. And here, shining [in] the morning, was a city with colored houses and dewy cobblestones all, a city without a broken stone. People lived there as they lived here, ate in dining rooms, slept in beds, went to school or work, to theater and church. They rode in buses or walked on the boulevard with canes or parasols. Amiens, I repeat was the loveliest city on earth.

A narrow, dark canal wound through the city, passing under ancient arched ridges, eddying under leaded casements, lapping at the feet of little children who sat at a back doorstep, studying the water.

The old woman went clacking down the morning street with her basket of wet flowers; the cab driver dozed in his high seat; the waiter with long mustaches polished the window of the café with a white cloth. And, later the children of Amiens hurried to school, babbling in their foreign tongues. The blacksmith's anvil rang there.

Happy Amiens! When I walked down those cobblestones thirteen years ago, hungry, I caught the fragrance from the flower woman's basket. I sniffed the smell of warm bread as the bakeries opened. I knew my wineshop by the bouquet and the smell of omelets cooking. Marie was there. She was much older than I and probably didn't know me from one visit to another. But Marie was beautiful. She had dark eyes with a silvery luster, an oval, golden face and lovely arms. Her sleeves were always rolled up when she worked, stirring omelets, serving red wine, patting her favorites on the cheek and calling them endearing names.

I had friends in Amiens—old men who liked to talk about America and the wild Indians; old women who insisted on showing letters from their sons at the front; young girls, high school boys, who knew English and would show you where Peter the Hermit was born; where Caesar fought the Ambiani; where Jules Verne wrote; where the best pastry was—everything.

Amiens was beautiful. Its delights were simple, but it was paradise.

The last time I saw Amiens, as I say, was thirteen years ago, this month. It was not the Amiens I had grown to love. It was a foreign city. Horses galloped through the street with limbers banging and careening behind them. Grim columns marched down the boulevards. Overhead the black airplanes droned. Workmen frantically stacked bags of sand against the wall of the cathedral.

As I walked from the station that morning I saw fear upon the faces of men and women. Little children cowered in the folds of their mothers' skirts. Nobody spoke lightly. Nobody laughed. Speech was brief and harsh with consternation. For four years Amiens had escaped. And now the thunder sounded beyond a pall of smoke on the outskirts of the city. I went to see "The Angel." It seemed to me that its recess was darker than ever before. It seemed to me that its beautiful head was bowed lower, that the little hands of stone more tightly clutched the hour glass and the skull, as if to stay time and death. I hurried out. A provost marshall stopped me and ordered me back to the front. All holidays had been cancelled in a sweeping order.

I shall you tell you little more –only this:

Five nights later I lay in a plowed field on the plains near Amiens. My feet were bleeding; I had marched five days through battle, in retreat. The British army was routed; behind us lay corpses and smoking devastation. I lay there in the cold, wet soil, shivering and exhausted. An airplane just had machine-gunned our column in the moonlight. We scattered and fell on our bellies in the field.

But I was not thinking of that. I was looking toward Amiens and the flames that towered there. I was listening to the distant thunder of its crumbling walls. I was listening to little children crying in the night.

Overhead a procession of enemy planes streamed with the roar across the stars. I saw that the endless procession had blotted a long strip of the firmament. I knew that the dark wing of death was sweeping across the city of loveliness.

I thought of the Weeping Angel, the little stone cherub, sitting there in the gloomy recess while the walls fell. One hand was upon the hourglass, the other upon a skull. Oh, time and death!

Obituary

Kansas City Star, October, 1959

It Happened in Kansas City

To the old timers the death of Hubert Kelley brings memories of the spectacular reporter of a quarter of a century ago. With a sharp pang the old timers realize that Hubert Kelley is now one of the newspaper legends of long ago, one to be mentioned along with Steve O'Grady and the few others who in their time brought a sense of drama to the readers of *The Star.*

The active Legionnaires of World War I remember Hubert Kelley through the droll characters of Pig Iron the Bugler who broke into humorous print with every American Legion convention and events concerning the armed forces.

Nationally he may be remembered by the readers of the old American Magazine of the late 1930s and early 1940s.

But a large part of his impact on Kansas City came through the anonymous stories of daily events. Through his interviews the public saw important Kansas City visitors as vivid as the characters of fiction. Through his eyes the readers saw more drama in public gatherings and other events than most persons who had witnessed them at first hand.

The old timers of *The Star* remember Hubert Kelley as a compelling person. When reporters gathered around the glasses late at night, he brought fire to the conversation.

His black eyes glowed with the excitement of events and people. From his conversation great characters emerged in quick succession, statesmen, preachers, bums and the strange economic quacks of the zany 1930s.

Hubert was one of the few persons born with the power to see the unusual story and to tell it. A reporter holds the unique responsibility of the public's eyes in the unfolding panorama of events. Hubert Kelley went on to be managing editor and editor of national magazines, but we think of him particularly as a brilliant example of a great generation of reporters.

October 6, 1959

Hubert (smiling, immediate left of Will Rogers, center), Kansas City, MO

Afterword

Hubert W. Kelley wrote many poems after the war, but his livelihood came from newspaper reporting, writing magazine articles, and ghost-writing pieces that appeared in *American Magazine* and, later in his life, *Reader's Digest*. He penned articles for J. Edgar Hoover, Eddie Rickenbacker, and Shirley Temple's mother. He covered the birth of the Dionne Quintuplets and interviewed Albert Einstein.

I believe he was permanently affected by his war experience. He married three times and had several affairs. Each marriage bore two children, a total of five sons and one daughter. He suffered a stroke in 1946, right before his fourth son was born, and although he lived another thirteen years, he was partially paralyzed and had difficulty working. He left two young boys from his third marriage when he died. He abandoned each of his marriages when his children were very young.

He was a teller of tales. He had his various families believing that he was part Native American and that Tennessee Williams was a cousin. I was told this story and almost approached the famous playwright in Sardi's one night before I learned it wasn't true. Perhaps Kelley once believed it because his mother's great-grandfather was rumored to have been captured while fighting at the Battle of Blue Licks with Daniel Boone. He was fifteen years old and adopted by a squaw but escaped after a time.

Above all, Kelley was remembered by all as a fine reporter and a good editor.

He was a heavy drinker and loved too many women, none very well. With the support of DeWitt Wallace, publisher of the *Reader's Digest*, he kept writing until shortly before he died. One is happy for what he accomplished, sad that he could not do more.

Unpublished article for *American Magazine* about WWII impact on France, written ca. 1945

Typed at the top: "OK, if and as approved by Department of State:"

There has been an impression in the United States and even among many Americans in the European theater that France suffered comparatively little material and moral damage as a result of her war and four years of German occupation. This misconception of the true state of affairs inside this ravaged country was not created by design on anybody's part. The French are a proud people. They present their best face to the world even though they are impoverished, hungry and without most of the necessities of life. They maintain their properties scrupulously and ingeniously, wear their clothes well, and deport themselves with dignity and courtesy. It is no wonder then, when our armies entered the larger cities, that Americans were deceived by the scenic surfaces of which the French are such masters.

If you visit Paris today you will be amazed and bewildered at the style of women on the street. But if you look again you may see that the finery is threadbare and patched and that the smart shoes are merely cloth with soles of wood, small protection in rainy winter weather. Shining shop windows display all manner of attractive apparel, perfume, and sport goods. But if you go inside, you will discover that the window is merely "a front", that stocks are almost exhausted, that what is offered may be of inferior quality. In the poorer quarters of Paris and in the Provinces, you see neither finery nor any merchandise to speak of. After all, most of the people of France live in the Provinces.

When the *American Magazine* asked me to inform the readers of the real conditions inside France, I consented to do so in the belief that a discussion of the unspeakable damage done to France will help us deal more adequately with the German people after their surrender, and to do everything possible to restore France, as well as other liberated countries to strength and prosperity. A strong and prosperous France is to our advantage.

The staggering part of this job I have undertaken is the difficulty of obtaining information of what the real conditions are, an indication in itself of the confused state of affairs left by the enemy when France was liberated. In the latter days of the occupation, the Germans forbade the publication of statistics. Employers and farmers in many cases falsified their production figures to protect their workers from deportation to German industries, and to obtain more raw materials Health statistics were kept from the world because the toll of malnutrition was so great.

Through the years of the occupation, one report states, tuberculosis increased four times. The birth rate declined; infant mortality increased.

With the limited information available, pieced together from reports of the army and French ministries, we do know that, contrary to general belief, the devastation in France today is far greater than that of 1914-18. It has been estimated that at least 900,000 homes and buildings have been destroyed by bombing attacks. In the North of France, I have been told, about million persons still are without homes. They live as best they can – in barns of neighbors and friends, in improvised shacks made of debris, and some families, less fortunate, sleep in the woods, in haystacks or merely wader from place to place, seeking shelter wherever they can find it. With a fuel shortage, due to lack of transportation, even city dwellers are suffering and sickening from the cold. In all Paris there are only a few hotels with heat. Consider the plight of those who, in the devastated areas, have no roof above their heads.

Courageous and resourceful, the French people are bringing order, security, and comfort to their dispossessed as rapidly as possible, but progress is slow because the mainsprings of the commonwealth have been severed by the war. In the first place, they have very little or now raw materials available to put their factories to work and permit even the essential movement of goods into centers of population. What raw materials are available cannot be moved from the sources of supply because of the widespread destruction of transportation facilities.

At the end of September, 1944, when the Germans left France, it is estimated that of 115,200 railway locomotives operating on French railways in 1938, only 10,200 were left in the country and of these 7,500 were damaged. Many of the locomotives in use were dangerously in need of replacement parts and repair. A few, made in Austria, bore manufacturer's stamps as old as 1865. Almost one half of the nation's freight cars were destroyed or had disappeared, presumably into German territory. More than 50 percent of railway installations were destroyed or rendered unusable, marshaling yards were blasted and burned, some 1,900 bridges, tunnels and other railway construction projects were blown up, and the whole French railway system paralyzed. Much of the damage was done by our own aerial bombing, a necessary step in the liberation of France.

While the French government and our own army engineers are rapidly restoring important lines and bridges, total freight movements, commercial and military, as I write, have reached only 28 percent of the average car loadings and 2 percent of train movements reported in 1938. One need only to fly crisscross above France today to understand the problem. Giant bridges, like toys, lie toppled in the Seine, the Loire, and the other great rivers of the country. Square miles of rail yards, round houses, and freight cars are razed and charred. Hence, this summer, crops rotted in orchards and fields because they could be moved. Mines, in some cases, could not be opened because pit props could not be shipped in from the timberlands. When winter came, very few hotels in Paris were able to procure fuel and hot water was seldom available. In thousands of French homes, there was no heat at all, little food, and threadbare clothing.

I believe there is a widespread belief in America today that, after D-day and liberation, we poured vast quantities of food and other necessities onto the Continent. We did what we could, but that has been little indeed. To the French, naturally enough, liberation in the first delirium of joy, meant the end of the war.

It was not until several weeks later that the vast task ahead was fully appreciated by the French. In fact, the first job was to beat the enemy back into German and destroy him there. The gigantic job of military supply and transportation taxed our every resource. It is still taxing it and, despite our great merchant marine and fleet, and the long lines of motor transport fumbling incessantly to the front, our armies are still short of many supplies. Under such circumstances French civilian supplies must unfortunately be greatly restricted in amount. This situation the French face sadly but bravely, and with their limited railways and motor transport are distributing what goods they can. Agriculture is satisfactory in most of France; there is not too little food. But the problem of transport makes it impossible to distribute this food properly. Moreover agriculture must suffer greatly if fertilizer is not returned to the soil. The Germans by their increasing demand for food taxed the soil to the limit.

When we entered France most of the ports were unusable. Docks and warehouses were demolished. The harbors were impassable with sunken ships. The port situation is still critical. Ships cannot bring in military supplies fast enough; we cannot unload them fast enough when they arrive. Hence, it has been impossible to bring into the nation the raw materials, foods and commodities needed to relieve the situation. It is a problem which must be solved if serious consequences are to be avoided.

France has lost a large part of her shipping. She estimates that of 3,000,000 tons of pre-war shipping, she ahs only 960,000 tons still left. This has been placed in the Allied pool. But she cannot build new ships. All her shipyards are destroyed and she could not move raw materials to the yards if it were possible to build.

Consider the effect of this vicious circle on industry. It is no wonder then that in France today, it is estimated that there are 600,000 unemployed workers, including 300,000 for the Paris area alone. There no doubt would be many more if were not for the part-time make-work program of the government, which helps maintain workers who lost their jobs through the bombing of factories or resistance sabotage by the workers themselves.

The industrial situation in France is most critical. Most of the factories not put out of operation by bombing have been closed for lack of raw materials. Even when raw materials are available, many cannot resume work because their machinery is so run down that it would not last a month. The German used it to the maximum and seldom replaced a worn part. It was only because of the careful husbandry and resourcefulness of the French workers that any of it continues to run at all. With a shortage of machine tools and machinery in a woeful state of disrepair, French industry cannot reproduce itself. It must look for machinery abroad. And it cannot approach normal production until it gets it. The total industrial production index for France in November has been roughly estimated at not more than 55 percent for France in 1943.

It is easy to see then how restless the French worker has become. Those who are working find their money of little value. The best figures we can obtain show that money wages have been raised since liberation only 50 percent, or about 260 percent of pre-war wages, while the official maximum prices are roughly estimated at 300 percent of pre-war wages. Black market supplementary prices, which even the poor must sometimes pay in emergencies, are sometimes as high as 700 percent of pre-war prices. But even with this deficiency in income the French are eating better today that when the Germans occupied the country. We furnish our own food, whereas the occupying Germans not only lived off the land but exported French goods to Germany. Our men in uniform are forbidden each in French restaurants, because that would be taking food from the mouths of French civilians. So the French today, even with paralyzed transport, according to one calculation, receive about 1,500 calories a day against 900 a day during the German occupation. The normal minimum is something above 3,000 calories a day.

Prices for consumers' goods are very high indeed, and more of the French seem able to pay them. They are certainly high in consideration of the exchange value of the franc – about 50 francs to one American dollar. Some soldiers and civilian workers have complained of the high prices of French goods due in part to the high rate for the franc. There may be a very few such cases, but, in fact, the French suffer also, due largely to scarcity of supplies. The devaluation of the franc might somewhat increase the purchasing power of American soldiers and salaried workers in France. However, it must be borne in mind that this is an economy of scarcity.

We clothe and feed our groups and provide them with as many of the luxuries of life as transportation will permit. They are in France but they are subsisting on another economic world, which, despite all its sacrifices, cannot even imagine the suffering and deprivations endured by the French people today. The exchange value of the franc was fixed by the French themselves to protect the pitiable remnants of its stocks and supplies.

The monetary situation in France is little understood in America today, but nowhere are the disastrous effects of German occupation more evident than in the financial field. In the first place (again my figure is a rough estimate) the German occupation cost France something like 1,300,000,000,000. francs, an inconceivable amount. That is a bill which France is paying out of her economy. As I write, posters advertising the first French liberation loan are flaring throughout Paris and motor cars with loudspeakers urge the people to subscribe. Citizens are responding patriotically in the cites, but the problem of communications and transport so far have interfered with the conduct of the campaign in rural areas.

The financial problems with which the Provisional Government is faced are large and difficult of solution. The Germans used the most highly refined techniques not only for carrying out their immediate objective of using the French economy, even to the point of exhaustion, to support the German war effort, but not further their long-range plan to enslave the French and to seize and control all their institutions.

Many Americans have felt that there is an inconsistency between the charge that the Germans looted France and the frequently repeated statements that the Germans paid for everything they took. There is no inconsistency here at all. Rather than forcibly wrest money and treasure from millions of French individuals, thus precipitating rebellion, the Germans took the francs from the nation and paid off the individuals. The individual appeared to be enriched while the nation, which supported the currency, was impoverished. No more vicious method of undermining a people's economic power has ever been devised.

The magnitude of German and German inspired expenditures in France can be seen from the fact that of a total French budget of 451.5 billion francs in 1943, 218.5 billion Francs were made up of occupation costs–almost one-half for the support of the invader. From the French point of view this expenditure was wholly unproductive it represented worthless paper given by the Germans in exchange for food and goods needed by the French at home, and for artworks and other lasting treasures to be carted back to Germany. Remember that this drain on the French treasury had been going on for years at the time of liberation. In addition, the French treasury had to bear the burden of the deficit in the Franco German clearing account, which mounted steadily throughout the occupation. The French treasury in effect had to finance the very pillage of its own nation. The clearing account deficit alone was 11.5 billion francs in 1941; 63.3 billion for 1943, and nearly 40 billion for the first six months of 1944.

This tremendous unproductive government expenditure was met largely by advances from the Bank of France and other forms of borrowing. In order to meet the demands of the Treasure, the Bank of France was required to print increasing quantities of bank notes which were poured into circulation at a steadily mounting rate. Circulation increased from approximately 123 billion francs in June, 1939, to about 600 billion francs at the time liberation. Thus, while the French people were having more and more francs to put into their pocketbooks, they were seeing their country despoiled of anything to spend them for. The disproportion between money and goods, which I have mentioned before, became a factor of overwhelming importance in France. It still is.

While France is struggling to get her industries running again, her ports open, her transport system functioning and her cities fed, the Government must continue to meets its obligations, pay its salaries, and keep the monetary system in operation. At the same time, it must make every effort to prevent inflation. And all of this with few taxes coming in from any source. Without industry and without individual incomes, taxes will be negligible.

It does not take any expert to see that the French government has a herculean task ahead. The French people can solve it, but not without the greatest understand and sympathy from other nations.

The needs of France are colossal. The larger part of her immediate wants she is seeking in her own colonies. In the meantime, she has compiled a longer range inventory of her needs which she hopes to fill by next June. And of 3,500,0000 tons of raw materials she is seeking, she is trying to buy 1,384,933 tons in the United States and Canada alone. She wants food, rubber, steel, chemicals, agricultural machinery, fertilizer, paper and pulp, fats and soap – basic things with which to regain her self-sufficiency and her power to produce part of the wealth of the world.

Once the shipping problem is solved, she will be confronted with a new problem – manpower shortage. The German robbed the French not only of goods and treasures. They even seized and deported 700,000 skilled workers – the lifeblood and genius of industrial production - in addition to 915,000 uniformed prisoners of war and 250,000 other French soldiers transformed into workers.

Altogether, including political and racial prisoners and citizens of Alsace, the Vosges, and Lorraine, German is holding almost 3,000,000 Frenchmen. Most of them are comparatively young, at the vital and productive age. And this out of a pre-war population of only 41, 928, 000. Today the population of France is estimated at only 38 million persons.

This brings us to one of the most delicate aspects of the whole situation inside France – the wrong that was done to her people morally and spiritually. It fills me with emotion to touch upon it, particularly when it involves a people as wise, sensitive, proud, and great as the French.

How many of my friends have said, on returning to Paris after liberation: "What has happened? This is not Paris. People seem bewildered, detached, or somnolent. I don't know what it is, but some shadow has fallen over their spirit."

At the same time, other persons, less cognizant of the nature of France, observed perfume in show windows, heard laughter and music from the doorways of night-clubs, marked thee stylish habiliments on the principal streets.

"The French have not been hurt," they said. "It is still gay Paris."

Some news stories reflected this latter point of view.

And to make matters worse, some Americans expressed doubts, even in the presence of their French friends, that German atrocities, now coming to light, were as terrible as the French portrayed. It was an unhappy circumstance. The French, feeling insecure in a hostile world, were profoundly shocked that even their past sufferings should be doubted.

I doubt whether there is a man, woman, or child in France today who has not been touched, to a greater or less degree, by the cruel and defiling hand of the invader. Most families have seen their loved ones deported, wounded in battle, tortured by the Gestapo, or insulted or intimidated in public places and on the streets. There is no myth about it. It is not part of a campaign of hate such as gave birth in the last war to untrue stories of atrocities committed by the Germans in Belgium. The French are so deeply wounded spiritually by what happened this time that many of them are ashamed to talk about it.

The climax of German brutality was the atrocity in the French town of Cradour-sur-Glans, near Limoges, which members of our armed forces have investigated. They believe it. They found indisputable evidence that it occurred.

On June 10, 1944, a German SS unit entered the town, lined up all the men in the village and shot them, then forced all the women and children into a church. The church was burned. Some 1,100 persons – the entire population of the town – were murdered that day, 800 of them women and children. Why? Nobody knows. The Germans never gave a satisfactory explanation of the event. Many thought it was some kind of reprisal.

The rest of this article is missing.